The Senior High School Principalship

Volume II: The Effective Principal

Richard A. Gorton

Kenneth E. McIntyre

National Association of Secondary School Principals
1904 Association Drive • Reston, Virginia 22091

About the authors:

Richard A. Gorton is chairman, Department of Administrative Leadership at the University of Wisconsin-Milwaukee. Kenneth E. McIntyre is professor, Department of Educational Administration at the University of Texas.

ISBN 0-88210-094-7

Copyright 1978

All Rights Reserved

National Association of Secondary School Principals

1904 Association Drive, Reston, Va. 22091

Contents

Foreword   v

1. Design of the Study   1

2. Personal, Professional, and School Characteristics   5

3. The Task Areas   13

4. The Nature of the Job   25

5. Solving Problems and Causing Change.   35

6. Professional Views and Assessments   43

7. The Effective Principal.   55

   Appendix

      A. The Interview Guide — Principals   64

      B. The Interview Guide — Significant Others   85

**Steering Committee
for the
Study of the Senior High School Principalship**

Lloyd E. McCleary
Richard A. Gorton
Judith S. Greene
Brother Eagan Hunter
Henry L. Miller
Eugene R. Smoley
Scott D. Thomson, *Chairman*

Research Team for the Study

Lloyd E. McCleary, *Chairman*
Richard A. Gorton
Kenneth E. McIntyre
David R. Byrne
Scott D. Thomson

Supported by the Rockefeller Family Fund

Foreword

MOST EVERYONE AGREES that the principal is the key to a good school. Yet few data have been collected on the senior high school principalship since 1965 when NASSP conducted and published its last national study.

The nature of the principalship surely has changed during the past decade in response to the many forces acting upon high schools in the late 1960s and early 1970s. Certainly the emergence of professional negotiations, of court decisions on student affairs and on desegregation, and the constantly shifting priorities of the public for schools presaged a different principalship in the late 1970s than existed in the mid 1960s.

Considering these circumstances and the importance of the position, NASSP decided that high priority must be given to a 1977 national study of the principalship so that the current nature of the assignment as well as the background and training of principals could be determined. Consequently, a steering committee was formed under the chairmanship of Deputy Executive Director Scott Thomson to launch the study.

Supporting funds were pledged by the Rockefeller Family Fund and the research team went to work. The steering committee and research team agreed that the study should consist of three parts: a random sample survey of 1,600 principals, an in-depth interview with 60 "effective" principals, and a look at future forces and conditions acting upon the principalship. This publication, Volume II, reports and analyzes data from the on-site interviews with 60 effective principals.

The study could only be completed with the cooperation of 60 highly professional and dedicated principals. We express our appreciation to them for taking time from their busy schedules to be interviewed, and also for arranging interviews for the research staff with students, parents, and central office personnel in their school districts.

A special note of thanks goes to the steering committee, to Lloyd McCleary as leader of the research team, and to Richard Gorton and Kenneth McIntyre as authors of this volume.

We believe this 1977 in-depth study of 60 effective principals brings an important new dimension to our understanding of the principalship. It documents the characteristics and behaviors which allow principals to be effective leaders in that highly complex institution, the American High School.

Owen B. Kiernan
Executive Director
NASSP

1 Design of the Study

DURING THE PLANNING PHASE for the 1977 study of the senior high school principalship, a decision was made not only to survey by questionnaire a large random sample of principals, but also to investigate the nature of "effective" principals. NASSP felt it was important to collect normative data about the typical senior high school principal, but strong support also existed for a parallel study that would focus upon the effective or exemplary principal.

Consequently, the research team, upon approval of the steering committee, developed selection criteria and interview instruments for this second project. The study involved interviews with principals and four groups of "significant others": students, parents, teachers, and central office/board of education personnel. The interviews were structured according to the instruments included in the Appendix.

Purpose, Sample, Selection

The purpose of the study was to ascertain the personal characteristics, professional qualities and competencies, and situational conditions which seem to be associated with effective, exemplary senior high school principals.

The sample for the study included 60 senior high school principals from across the United States. They were identified through the use of a reputational selection process which employed these criteria:

- The school appears to be focused in direction and moving to achieve its purposes.

- The school leadership anticipates emerging problems and acts in an informed way to resolve them.

- The school includes community persons in the development of goals and objectives.

- The school involves youth with learning in an adult community.

- The school climate is supportive and reflects high morale.

In order to obtain a sample representing different conditions and situations, four population classifications were used:

Urban—Has a population of 185,000 or more. The city in which the school is located is recognized as a major population center by the U.S. Bureau of the Census, and as the center of what is defined by the Bureau of the Budget as a Standard Metropolitan Statistical Area (SMSA).

Suburban—Is located near (roughly 30 miles) a major urban city and is included in the urban city's particular SMSA.

Medium City—Has a population of 29,000–160,000, not fitting into the above categories, but still a definite center of population.

Rural—Has a population below 12,000—a very small center of population not close (within 100 miles) to any larger center of population.

The selection process included these steps:

1. A letter describing the purpose of the study and the selection criteria was sent to the director of secondary education in the Department of Public Instruction in each state, requesting the nomination of at least two principals for each of the four population categories. A similar letter was sent to the executive secretary of each of the state associations of secondary school principals and to professors of school administration in each of the states.

2. A pool of more than 300 nominees emerged from step one, with 102 principals being nominated independently by at least two of the above sources. From this double nominee group came the principals included in the final screening.

3. Verifications of nominations were made by telephoning the superintendents of each of the 102 principals to determine whether or not local effectiveness matched state-wide reputation. Superintendents were asked, "Would you place this person high on the list of effective and exemplary principals in your district?" Three nominees were dropped from consideration because of doubts expressed during these conversations.

2

A final group of 62 principals, with consideration given to a balance of geographical, community, and school size factors, constituted the subjects invited to participate in the study. Two persons declined to cooperate, leaving the 60 principals who comprise the group for study.

Since the research team wanted to study exemplary principals from several perspectives, each of the principals in the sample was asked to identify student, teacher, parent, and central office representatives, according to type of leadership position, who would be knowledgeable about the performance of the principal. In addition to being interviewed for about three hours by a member of the research team, each principal was asked to arrange for interviews with the four groups of "significant others."

Specific leadership roles were identified for each referent group; for instance, the students interviewed represented: (1) the editor of the school paper; (2) the student body or senior class president; (3) the president of a vocationally oriented club; and (4) the president of an academically oriented club. The teachers interviewed represented: (1) president of the teachers' group at the school; (2) the English chair; (3) the business education chair; and (4) a non-tenure teacher.

It is important to note that the study did not intend to identify the "one best principal" in each state. To the research team, such an identification is neither possible nor desirable. The study does identify, however, persons who represent the most effective principals in each state according to the criteria defined by the research team and applied by the nominators.

Instrumentation, Data Collection, Analysis

After consideration of possible alternatives, the research team decided that a structured interview would be the most appropriate method for collecting information from the effective principals and from the "significant others." The questions for these were developed after a review of the literature and several pilot tests of the instruments. The final version of the 25-page interview guide for the principal contained the following major sections:

- Principal—School Information
- Principal—Personal Information
- The Job
- Students, Community/Parents, Staff, Curriculum/Programs, and Program Evaluation
- Problem Solving and Problem Attack
- Change
- Personal/Professional
- Future

3

The interview guide for the "significant others" paralleled the principals' guide, for the most part, in Sections 3 through 7.

The interviews were conducted during a one-and-a-half to two-day site visit by a member of the research team or a professional associate. The principals' interviews typically lasted three to five hours; the interviews with each group of "significant others" took one to two hours. Interview responses were recorded in writing, and in a number of cases were supplemented by tape recordings.

The data from all the interviews were subjected to content analysis by a group of doctoral students and faculty members at the University of Utah, with later supplementary analyses by the writers of this report when necessary. The major findings of the study are reported in the chapters that follow.

4

2 Personal, Professional, and School Characteristics

THE 60 EXEMPLARY PRINCIPALS ranged in age from 33 to 59, the mean age being 43.9. Fifty-four of the 60 were males, and 53 of the 60 were white. The remaining seven were black. Fifty-three were married, six were single, and the marital status of one was unknown. Of the six single principals, four were priests or nuns serving in parochial schools.

Professional Characteristics

Training

All the principals had bachelor's degrees, earned between the years 1940 and 1973. The major fields were:

Bachelor's Degree Field	Number of Principals
Business	2
Education	9
Humanities	9
Industrial Arts	2
Physical Education	7
Physical/Biological Sciences	14
Social Sciences	18
	61 (one principal reported two bachelor's degrees)

In addition to their bachelor's degrees, all the principals had master's or higher degrees, earned between the years 1946 and 1975. The major fields were:

Master's Degree Field	Number of Principals
Educational Administration	30
Education	12
Humanities	3
Physical Education	4
Physical/Biological Sciences	5

(continued on next page)

5

Master's Degree Field	Number of Principals
Social Sciences	3
Guidance	3
Counseling	2
Law	1
	63 (four reported two master's degrees; one reported a doctorate but no master's)

Ten principals held education specialist degrees earned between 1956 and 1977—eight in educational administration, one in guidance, and one in counseling.

Eighteen reported Ed.D. or Ph.D. degrees, earned between 1964 and 1977—13 in educational administration, four in education, and one in counseling/special education.

As undergraduates, most of the future principals engaged in a wide variety of activities. Although 12 listed no activities, 38 listed one or two, and 10 listed three or more activities. The most frequently named activities were:

College Activities	Number of Principals
Athletics	36
Student Government	11
Music	6
Drama	5
Student Newspaper	3

Twenty of the 60 reported membership in fraternities or sororities, and several others listed clubs and other student organizations.

Scholarships, prizes, and various other honors and awards were typical of the undergraduate experiences of many principals. Two-thirds of the group reported at least one, and 12 of the 60 listed three or more honors or awards. No one category was named by more than five of the principals. Somewhat surprisingly, only five were graduated cum laude and only two were members of Phi Beta Kappa.

Career Patterns

All 60 of the principals had taught early in their careers. Ten had also been involved in the coaching of athletics, 10 in guidance or counseling (including two who had been in coaching as well as guidance/counseling), and six in department chairmanships. This teaching and teaching-related experience consumed a total of six years or fewer for 30 of the 60 principals. Few of the principals had taught more than 12 years. Other than teaching or the related fields mentioned above, no single type of experience prior to school administration was reported by more than one or two of the principals.

By far the most common route to the senior high school principalship, after classroom teaching, was the assistant principalship (or vice principalship). Thirty-four of the principals reported this type of experience—23 for a period of one-three years, seven for a period of four-six years, and four for a period of seven-nine years.

Fifteen of the 60 had served as elementary or junior high school principals (mostly the latter) prior to their appointment to the senior high school principalship. Four of these persons served as assistant senior high school principals before entering the full principalship. Nine of the 60 had previously occupied central office positions such as director of adult education, director of activities, director of staff development, director of secondary education, or director of athletics. One had worked in a state department of education and one had been superintendent of a private school.

Full-time work experience outside of education, since the bachelor's degree, was reported by about half of the principals. Eighteen had military experience of some type, three had sold insurance, and two had been in building construction work. Several other lines of work were reported by individual principals; these included work as a lawyer, a professor, a professional football player, a professional baseball player, and a rancher.

Only four of the 60 principals entered their first principalship prior to 1960, the earliest being 1953. Two of the 60 became principals only one year prior to the present study. The median year of entering the first principalship was 1969. The median age of respondents was 35, with a range of 25 to 55.

Only four of the 60 principals had been teachers and administrators in the same school, although 20 had served in both capacities in the same district. Thirty-seven had held more than one administrative position in the same district—usually assistant principal and principal—although few reported more than one in the same school.

Inservice Training

7

The principals were asked to mention all voluntary inservice training programs in which they had engaged, totaling at least three days per program, since January 1973. Fourteen principals recalled no such training activities, 24 cited one or two activities, and 22 listed three or more.

The training activities that were named covered a wide range of topics. The activities were usually in the form of institutes, seminars, or workshops, and they were usually sponsored by universities or administrators' associations at the national or state level. The organization cited most often was the National Association of Secondary School Principals, for its National Institutes for Secondary School Administrators (listed by 20 principals). The National Academy for School Executives, sponsored by the American Association of School Administrators, was named by five principals. State-level activities were cited 17 times. Foundations were listed by eight principals (Kettering by five, Danforth by two, and Rockefeller by one).

The 60 principals were asked to indicate the professional organizations of which they were members, how active they were in each, and how useful the membership in each had been. Following are the organizations named by more than five principals, together with the responses to the questions dealing with involvement and usefulness:

PROFESSIONAL MEMBERSHIPS

Organization	Number of Principals	How Active Are You?			How Useful Is Membership?		
		Very	Moderately	Not	Very	Moderately	Not
NASSP	59	19	33	7	48	10	1
State Principals Association	53	32	15	6	33	16	4
Phi Delta Kappa	33	2	15	16	21	4	8
ASCD	26	2	13	11	9	9	8
AASA	24	1	7	16	2	8	14
Local Principals' Association	7	5	2	0	4	2	1

It appears that most of the 60 principals belong to their state and national associations, that they are at least moderately active in them—especially the state associations—and that they find their memberships to be quite useful. NASSP gets especially good marks. When the principals were asked specifically what contributed to the usefulness of their memberships, publications were cited most often.

Other Professional Activities

The principals were asked to state the professional activities (such as speaking, writing, teaching) in which they had been engaged since January 1973. The responses indicate that many of the principals are quite active in such endeavors. Only a few of the more common activities will be cited here.

Fourteen principals had given speeches at national conventions or conferences, 13 at the state level, 10 at universities or colleges, and three at the regional level. Several others had spoken at local gatherings.

Professional writing was less common, although nine had articles published in journals and one had authored a textbook.

Ten had taught courses in colleges or universities and six had operated workshops. Eight had served as consultants.

Several of the principals had been active as officers or committee members of state, regional, or national organizations.

Activity in Community Organizations

The principals were asked to list community organizations of which they were members, to state how active they were in each, and to indicate the usefulness of membership in each. Only seven of the 60 principals reported belonging to no such organizations. Eleven belonged to one, 19 to two, 11 to three, eight to four, and four principals belonged to five or more.

Church memberships were cited by 42 of the principals, 21 of whom were "very active" and 20 "moderately active." Twenty-eight of the 42 indicated that their church membership was "very useful" and the other 14 said "moderately useful."

Service clubs were listed by 27 principals, Rotary being most frequently named (by 11), followed by Kiwanis and Lions (by seven each). The principals generally indicated moderate to very active involvement in the service clubs, and found their membership to be either moderately or very useful.

Five principals listed the Chamber of Commerce, three listed the Civic Association, two listed the Community Action Council, and one was a member of the City Council. In most instances, involvement was moderate to very active, and moderately to very useful.

Other organizations listed by three or more principals were the Boy Scouts, Mental Health Association, YMCA, and NAACP. Involvement and usefulness were perceived to be "moderate" and "very."

Honors and awards for activities outside the schools were reported by several of the principals, although no one type of honor or award was listed by more than one principal. Service club awards of various kinds were cited, along with such honors as Chamber of Commerce Citizen of the Year, NAACP Brotherhood Award, Cultural Arts Committee Award, Business and Professional Women's Outstanding Achievement Award, Jaycee Distinguished Service Award, Urban League Distinguished Service Award, Who's Who—American Women, Who's Who in the West, Who's Who—Black Americans, and many others.

Characteristics of the Schools and Districts

The school districts represented in the study ranged from those in rural areas to those in large cities such as Detroit. The mean district enrollment of the public school systems (excluding Detroit) was slightly more than 21,000. The systems represented by the parochial schools also varied widely in enrollment, from 7,000 to 53,000, with a mean of approximately 26,000. The number of high schools ranged from one to 22 in the public school systems, with a mean of 4.28, and in the parochial school systems the range was from 14 to 31, with a mean of 25.

Enrollment in the 60 high schools involved in the study (including public and parochial schools) ranged from 400 to 3,100, with a mean of 1,480. As expected, the smaller schools were mostly in the rural areas; in fact, of the 14 high schools enrolling 1,000 or fewer students, 11 were in rural areas, one was in a medium-sized city, and the other two were parochial schools in urban areas. The largest schools (more than 3,000 students) were in both urban and suburban areas. Two out of three in the enrollment categories 2,201–3,000 were in suburban areas. The medium-sized high schools (enrolling 1,000–2,200) were fairly evenly divided among urban, suburban, and medium-sized city categories.

The "typical" high school employed 72 full-time teachers, five part-time teachers, and four full-time counselors. In addition, 43 of the high schools employed part-time teachers (mean of 5.03), and 15 high schools employed part-time counselors (mean of 1.90).

All 60 principals reported having at least some assistance from assistant principals, deans, activity directors, and the like. The range was from one half-time assistant to a staff of 11 administrative persons, as shown below:

SIZE OF ADMINISTRATIVE STAFF

Number on Administrative Staff	Number of Principals Reporting
.5	1
1.0	4
1.5	1
2.0	6
2.5	2
3.0	23
3.5	1
4.0	2
4.5	2
5.0	11
6.0	4
7.0	1
8.0	1
11.0	1

Surprisingly little relationship exists between school size and number of persons on the administrative staff, except for the schools in rural areas, which tended to be smallest and to have the least administrative help. For example, in the 1,401 to 1,800 enrollment classification, size in the urban areas ranged from two to 11, and in the suburban areas the range was from three to six. There was a tendency for the suburban schools to be relatively well staffed; for example, 40 percent of the principals in suburban schools had five or more administrative staff members, compared with only 29 percent of the principals in urban areas—even though the urban schools tended to be larger.

Perceptions of the adequacy of assistance available through administrative staff varied somewhat according to school category, as shown below:

PERCEPTIONS OF ADEQUACY OF ADMINISTRATIVE HELP

	Area			
	Urban	Suburban	Med.-Sized	Rural
Completely Adequate	10 (48%)	7 (47%)	6 (50%)	3 (25%)
Usually Adequate	9 (43%)	5 (33%)	6 (50%)	5 (42%)
Somewhat Inadequate	2 (9%)	2 (13%)	—	1 (8%)
Completely Inadequate	—	1 (7%)	—	(25%)

Most of the principals seem to be pleased with the assistance they have. Evidently those in rural areas are least satisfied with the amount of administrative help available to them; of course, they have the least help, but their schools are the smallest. Principals in the medium-sized cities are either "completely" or "usually" satisfied. Principals in the suburban areas are somewhat less satisfied with the amount of administrative help than are the principals in the urban areas, even though the suburban schools are relatively well staffed.

The department chairperson is another source of administrative assistance in three-fourths of the high schools represented in the study. The number of such persons with at least one period of released time per day for administrative duties ranged from one to 16, with a mean of 8.20. Most of the principals regarded the assistance received from this source to be "usually" or "completely" adequate.

Student Body   11

The racial-ethnic composition of the student bodies of the 60 schools varied widely within each community category as well as among the total sample of schools. However, certain differences can be detected when schools in the four community types are compared.

Following are the percentages of schools in which more than nine-tenths of the students were white: urban, 33 percent; suburban, 60 percent; medium-sized city, 25 percent; and rural, 75 percent. On the other hand, four of the 60 schools—two urban and two suburban—had student bodies of which more than nine-tenths of the students were black.

Only five of the schools had student bodies that were 10 percent or more Chicano. Two schools had appreciable numbers of students of Asian origin (11 percent and nine percent), and four had significant numbers of American Indian students (20 percent, 16 percent, 10 percent, and eight percent).

Programs

When asked what percentage of the student body was enrolled in certain types of programs, the principals gave responses indicating great differences among the 60 schools. For example, three principals indicated that more than 90 percent of the students are in college preparatory programs, but three other principals said that 20 percent or less are in such programs. The median for college preparatory programs was in the 51-60 percent category.

Percentages in vocational/business programs ranged from five percent or less in three schools to 71-80 percent in one school. The median for vocational/business programs was in the 21-30 percent category.

Percentages in general programs ranged from five percent or less in two schools to 81-90 percent in two schools. The median for general programs was in the 11-20 percent category.

Another question dealt with percentages of junior and senior students in various community experience programs. The following table shows the number of principals reporting various percentages of students in different community experience programs:

PERCENTAGE OF JUNIORS AND SENIORS IN
COMMUNITY EXPERIENCE PROGRAMS

Percentage	Work-Study	Released Time	Community Service	Alternative Programs	Other
91–100			1		
81–90				1	
71–80					
61–70	1				
51–60	1	1			
41–50		3	1		
31–40		2	1	1	
21–30	3	2			
11–20	17	7	4	2	3
6–10	15	9	7	7	2
1–5	15	17	19	18	6

3 The Task Areas

ALMOST ALL OF THE PRINCIPALS stated that they meet regularly with student leaders. The frequency of the meetings is about evenly divided among the following categories: daily, weekly, biweekly, and monthly. The "significant others" were evidently not completely aware of these meetings, especially the daily ones, which very few of the students, teachers, parents, or superintendent/school board leaders mentioned. Students and teachers were more prone to report "no regular meetings" than were parents and superintendent/school board leaders.

The student leaders with whom the principals meet most frequently are student council officers, class officers, club leaders, and informal leaders, in that order. The "significant others" tended to agree with the principals on this.

The typical content of such meetings in recent months, according to the principals, pertained to extracurricular activities and projects, followed by school rules, student discipline, relations among students, and curriculum matters. All of the "significant others" agreed with the principals that extracurricular activities and projects constituted the main content of the principal-student leader meetings. Student behavior was mentioned frequently by all of the "significant others." The superintendent/school board leader groups tended to report more content relating to student government than did the principals of the other groups.

Principals were asked how they influenced student behavior in positive directions. They tended to report using positive methods themselves and also working through others, usually the faculty or the student activities director. Principals' efforts generally fall into one or more of three categories: (1) dealing with problems or conditions that arise; (2) establishing and maintaining participation and responsibility, and setting higher standards and expectations; and (3) developing new practices or activities.

Communication with students is a key element in the principals' strategies. Both formal and informal channels of communication are utilized through student leaders and directly to classes, groups, and the

13

total student body. Many principals stressed the importance of being visible, visiting with students in a positive, enthusiastic manner. Involving students and giving them responsibility are crucial. When things go right, the student body should get much of the credit. When they go wrong, problems should not be dodged or covered up, but dealt with in an open and positive manner.

Specific tactics for problem resolution include surveying the situation, talking with individuals to get the facts, being open to suggestions, getting outside support, keeping the staff and central office informed, monitoring progress, giving reinforcement, treating students like adults, and showing real concern.

Principals use many of the above tactics to establish and maintain responsibility and higher standards, in addition to working on orientation programs, training students and faculty in participatory decision making, and confronting those who do not comply with rules.

The development of new practices or activities is the third type of activity cited by several of the principals as an attempt to influence student behavior in positive directions. Examples include restructuring student organizations; giving student leaders special responsibilities; and getting faculty and parents, as well as students, involved.

Principals tended to see themselves in one or two roles in implementing the initiatives previously discussed: initiator and facilitator. The role of initiator was suggested by such comments as "anticipate and influence the direction of planning," and "set policies and rules, and then follow through." The facilitator role was suggested by comments like "involve and be supportive of staff and students," "listen, talk, and share," "monitor all the way," "get and give feedback," "keep the program coordinated," and "be sure that everyone knows what is going on." The general impression is that these principals see themselves primarily as facilitators and that their initiator role is an important, but subtle, one.

As seen by the principals, the main school-connected concerns of their students were related to school activities (need for more activities, lack of school spirit, etc.), as well as matters related to instruction (poor teaching, grading practices, freedom in the classroom), and curriculum concerns (primarily preparation for college or jobs). Peer relationships were cited by several principals, and several mentioned students' wanting to be "treated like adults."

Student leaders' views of school-connected concerns reflected a greater concentration on the future—especially college and jobs—than was apparent in the principals' perceptions of students' concerns. Even the students' concerns about curriculum seemed to be associated with their future, academically and/or vocationally. A few students mentioned concerns pertaining to peer relations and social affairs, and a few others mentioned the lack of smoking areas at school.

Teacher, parent, and superintendent/board member perceptions of student concerns closely paralleled those of the students. Each group overwhelmingly cited getting prepared for college or jobs as the main concerns of students. A few mentioned school activities, smoking, and social relationships.

As the principals see them, the main nonschool concerns of students are related to money—for example, holding a job while going to school, especially in order to support an automobile. A few mentioned drugs and alcohol, family problems, boy-girl relations, and social issues, although the latter were often mentioned as *not* being important concerns of students at present. Getting into college and getting jobs were frequently given as both school and nonschool concerns.

When principals were asked how they kept informed about what students are thinking, they characteristically responded by referring to informal contacts—circulating among the students in the halls, in the cafeteria, at school activities, and the like. There was some mention of using the school newspaper, setting up advisory committees, and using other formal means, but the prevailing mode was reported to be informal conversations with the students.

Students, teachers, parents, and superintendents/school board members agree that the principals' means of keeping up with students' concerns are primarily informal ones. Each group also mentioned such sources as informal feedback from parents, teachers, and others; meetings with student groups; newspapers, letters, and other written means of communication; and questionnaire surveys of student opinion.

As the principals see it, their primary role, *vis-à-vis* the students, seems to be that of a listener, a standard setter, a friend, an advocate, and a model—someone who cares and demonstrates it behaviorally. The principals mentioned very few things that would appear in a formal job description.

The "significant others" were asked to comment on the role the principal plays in student activities and in discipline. With regard to the principal's role in student activities, the "others" see him as the final decision maker, as well as a monitor and facilitator. In those schools having a vice-principal in charge of student activities, the "significant others" view the principal largely as a booster and supporter. The principal attends most of the activities, especially the games, concerts, plays, and other events that attract crowds.

The role of the principal with respect to discipline is significantly influenced by the presence of a vice-principal in most of the schools that are large enough to have one or more. In most cases where there is a vice-principal, usually in charge of discipline, the principal has the final authority in dealing with major discipline problems and is involved in student appeals. The principal is generally viewed as a "firm but fair" person who doesn't spend a lot of his time on disciplinary matters because the school is well run.

Each group of "significant others" was asked to rate the principal with respect to the way in which he deals with students, on a five-point scale ranging from 1.0 (extremely autocratic) to 5.0 (extremely democratic). The ratings by all groups tended toward the democratic end of the scale. Nobody gave a principal a rating of 1.0. All four group medians were 4.0, indicating that the principals were perceived to be on the democratic side, but not extremely so.

Principals were asked: "How would you like to be perceived by students in your role as principal?" The responses ranged from the traditional authoritarian figure to the friend. The predominant response produced an image of the "firm but fair" leader, the open and honest helper, the mover who deals with problems and doesn't neglect them, the approachable friend who is humane and caring, the person who does everything possible to produce good schooling. In other words, the principals want to be seen as both people-oriented and product-oriented.

When asked what their schools' contributions should be to the lives of the students, the principals emphasized both personal fulfillment and the development of productive citizens who will serve society well. Neither the cognitive academic skills nor social maturation and the development of values should be slighted.

Community/Parents

Evidently most of the principals do not meet with groups of parents on a regular basis. Approximately one-third of the principals said that they do meet regularly with parent groups, with about equal numbers reporting such meetings with athletic or music booster clubs, parent advisory groups, parent-teacher or parent-student associations, or the executive committees of such associations. The frequency of meetings with parents varies from "frequently" or "as needed" to monthly or bimonthly. Monthly meetings are the most common.

The "significant others" groups tended to agree with the principals regarding the principals' meetings with parent groups. All of the "others" groups, as a whole, reported regular meetings with the PTA most frequently. Students and parents reported boosters' club meetings next most frequently, followed by parent advisory committees. Teachers and superintendent/school board leaders reversed the latter two types of meetings with respect to frequency. Generally speaking, all of the "others" agreed with the principals.

According to the principals, the main concerns of parent groups over the past several months have been in the general area of curriculum and program. Such specifics as the quality of college preparatory work, the "basics," and the quality of teaching were mentioned frequently. Another area of concern has been student behavior—discipline, drugs, attendance problems, and difficulties arising from desegregation. A third area of concern has been finance problems.

All the "significant others" groups agreed with the principals that curriculum and program concerns are the main ones that bring principals and parent groups together. Student behavior and problems of financing the schools were also mentioned by several of the groups.

The principals reported significant contacts with a wide range of community groups, but no one group was named by more than 10 percent of the principals. Of the civic clubs and service organizations, Rotary was named most (by six principals) followed by Kiwanis, Lions, Optimists, and Exchange. The main purpose of the contacts with these organizations is largely that of sharing information.

Six principals reported significant contacts with the Chamber of Commerce, and several mentioned church groups. Several other groups were mentioned by three or fewer principals.

When asked whether community groups or individuals participate in curriculum planning for the school, 40 percent responded in the affirmative. Where such participation does take place, the process is usually one of forming advisory groups which operate on an *ad hoc* basis. Several principals spoke of advisory groups for special programs such as vocational education.

The "significant others" groups were somewhat more inclined to say that the principals consult with community groups or individuals in curriculum planning than were the principals themselves. Slightly more than half of these groups, except for the teachers, reported that such consultations take place "often" or "sometimes." Forty-six percent of the teacher group responses fell into one of these categories. When asked how beneficial such meetings are, all the groups (except three of the student groups) indicated that the meetings are "very helpful" or "somewhat helpful." Parents were most positive of the "other" groups, with more than three-fourths responding in the "very helpful" category. Approximately two-thirds of the superintendent/school board and teacher groups responded "very helpful," as did slightly more than half of the student groups.

When the principals were asked in what other ways (other than curriculum) the school is influenced by community organizations, their responses indicated either informal contacts or the support or advocacy of specific programs by formal organizations or pressure groups. There was a tendency on the part of many principals to report that when things are going well the community shows little concern and has a minimum of influence on the school program.

The principals were asked in what areas they try to involve parents or other citizens in school affairs. One type of response dealt with involvement in processes such as curriculum planning, goal setting, fund raising, policy making (especially in matters related to students' rights and responsibilities), and evaluating the program. Another type of response dealt with the use of parents or other citizens as aides, resource persons, and helpers (especially in extracurricular activities).

Recent initiatives to increase parent or citizen participation were reported by a few principals. These included organizing citizen-student desegregation committees, booster clubs, and advisory groups; sending students to call on homes in the community; organizing coffee sessions and open group meetings; and contacting people on a one-to-one basis.

Methods employed to inform parents and the community in general include a wide variety of printed matter, such as newsletters (the most frequently reported method), newspaper articles, and special mailings. Other means are also used, including speeches and telephone calls. Methods that are used to get feedback from the citizenry are primarily informal ones—being accessible and listening—in addition to more formal avenues such as advisory councils, needs assessment procedures, and opinion surveys.

Each of the "significant others" groups was asked to rate the principal's effectiveness in working with parents and other citizens. The scale ranged from 1.0 (extremely ineffective), to 5.0 (extremely effective). The median ratings were all high: students, 4.0; teachers, 5.0; parents, 5.0; and superintendents/school board leaders, 4.5.

Staff

Most principals reported regular meetings with various staff groups, especially the entire faculty and the department chairpersons. A higher proportion of the urban principals spoke of such meetings than did the other groups. Fewer of the rural principals reported having meetings with department chairpersons than did the other categories of principals, probably because their "departments" often consist of one person not considered a "chairperson." The rural principals seem to depend mostly on meetings with the faculty as a whole.

Another frequently mentioned staff group in all but the rural schools is the cabinet or administrative staff. Less frequently mentioned staff groups included task forces, building committees, curriculum councils, and specific groups such as counselors and guidance personnel, secretaries, and teacher association representatives.

As to frequency of meetings of the faculty as a whole, the mode is once per month, followed by biweekly, bimonthly, and "as needed." Meetings of department chairpersons tend to be more frequent (biweekly being the model response), whereas meetings of the cabinet or administrative staff are most likely to be weekly.

The "significant others" groups tended to support the principals' reports concerning meetings with staff groups. All of the "significant others" mentioned the faculty as a whole and department chairpersons most frequently, together with a range of other responses. Teachers and superintendents/school board leaders frequently spoke of cabinet and administrative staff meetings.

What are the main issues or concerns of teachers in the high schools involved in this study? According to the principals, student

18

behavior (vandalism, crime, drug use, apathy, irrationality) is the main concern of the teachers, followed—in rank order—by salaries and negotiation problems, quality education (teaching environment, curriculum, criticisms of the educational program), insufficient time, class size, instructional materials, clerical help, and financial support.

The "significant others," including the teachers themselves, tended to see salaries as the main problem of teachers, followed by student behavior. Large class size was a distant third in the rankings. Other problems were mentioned, but far less frequently. There was considerable similarity in the rankings of the different "significant others" groups.

According to the principals, the main causes of good school morale and good school climate are closely associated with the actions of the principals themselves. Such actions are characterized by support of teachers in the performance of their duties, involvement of teachers in the making of decisions that are important to them, and open, honest communication at all times.

Principals were asked to cite specific initiatives that they had taken in the last three years to provide or improve faculty inservice education. No single pattern emerged from their responses. Some principals admitted having taken no such initiatives. Of those who had, the most common reported action was to set up a committee to determine needs and plan inservice training activities, and to provide resources to get the training accomplished.

Several principals spoke of long-range plans, including the assessment of needs, setting of school-wide priorities, and development of an annual plan to serve as a guide for departments in implementing the plan. Several others referred to their utilization of the school district's staff development resources, and several mentioned tying all improvement projects to inservice training in the belief that any fundamental change in the school almost always requires staff training.

What are the advantages and disadvantages of administering a school with a master contract or negotiated agreement? Several of the principals, particularly in the rural schools, said that no master contract was negotiated in their districts. Most of the principals in school districts with master contracts seem to favor them. Some of the cited advantages are that the contract clarifies rights, responsibilities, and procedures; provides support to administrative authority and takes the principal "off the hook"; provides security; improves salaries and working conditions; reduces capriciousness; and reduces conflicts.

On the other hand, cited disadvantages are that the contract reduces managerial prerogatives and limits the principal's freedom to act, sets up an atmosphere of antagonism between administration and faculty, fosters formal and impersonal relationships, and leads to the acceptance of minimum standards of performance.

Another question posed to the principals concerned their involvement in the process of negotiations with teachers. The principals' responses were placed on a five-point scale, from 1.0 (no involvement) to 5.0 (high involvement). Most of the principals stated that they are not involved at all. Of the 25 who did report involvement, the range was from 1.5 (almost none at all) to 5.0 (high involvement). Only eight of the principals perceived their involvement to be above 3.0.

The principals were asked how they thought their teachers perceived them in regard to their position in negotiations, and their responses were placed on a scale from 1.0 (not supportive) to 5.0 (highly supportive). Twenty-two of the principals said the question was not applicable to them. Of those who responded, the range was from 1.0 to 5.0, and the median was 3.75—slightly above the "somewhat supportive" level.

Asked to describe the issue and the process if a grievance had been filed in the school during the year, only 12 prinicpals reported any grievances. In most cases the process included filing the grievance, notifying the principal, appealing to the central office, and finally appealing to the board. The issues included a wide range of complaints such as class loads, assignment to duties, and evaluation of performance.

The principals and the "significant others" were also asked to characterize the faculty's influence in the decision-making process, on a five-point scale ranging from 1.0 (not at all influential) to 5.0 (highly influential). Although the range for the principals and all of the "significant others" groups was from 1.5 or 2.0 to 5.0, the median rating in every case was 4.0. There seems to be widespread agreement that faculties in the schools represented are influential in the decision-making process.

How effective are principals perceived to be in the area of staff relations? The principals gave self-ratings ranging from 3.0 (somewhat effective) to 5.0 (highly effective), with a median rating of 4.0. These ratings coincided exactly with those of both the teachers and the parents. The students and the superintendent/school board leaders gave the principals a median rating of 4.5.

20

Curriculum/Programs

It is evident from an analysis of the principals' responses that the curriculum development process in the 60 high schools is one in which departments, the high school faculty as a whole, and the central office are heavily involved. Generally speaking, the departments originate and develop the plans, prepare the materials, and do much of the evaluation; the faculty as a whole prioritizes goals, discusses plans, and reviews progress; and the central office provides district-wide goals and plans, consultant assistance, resources, and final approval.

Somewhat less prominent in the process are curriculum committees which assess needs, review proposals, and evaluate; cabinets or administrative councils which review proposals, plan inservice programs, and review outcomes; and consultants who provide ideas, conduct training, develop materials, and evaluate results.

According to the principals, outside resources that are used in the planning process are largely from universities or the district office, with a few mentions of regional centers, state agencies, and professional associations. Few "significant others" groups had enough knowledge of the process to discuss the questions, except for the superintendent/school board leaders, who mentioned central office participation very frequently, followed by university resources and professional associations.

In a few of the high schools students, parents, and community groups also participate in curriculum development. Students and parents assist in the assessment of needs and sometimes in planning. Parents and community groups sometimes request courses or programs and react to plans.

The "significant others" agreed with the principals in listing departments, the faculty as a whole, and the central office as the three main groups in the curriculum development process. The superintendent/school board groups indicated that central office personnel were the main participants in curriculum development, and the parent leaders agreed. Students saw the faculty as a whole to be paramount, and the teacher groups perceived the departments, faculty as a whole, and central office to be about equally involved, with a slight edge to the departments. There was a tendency for each "significant others" group to see its own constituents as being slightly prominent in the curriculum planning process; i.e., students tended to list students, teachers listed teachers, and parents listed parents.

Each of the "significant others" groups was asked to describe the process used by the principal in planning major events, projects, or programs. Most of the groups expressed considerable uncertainty, especially the students and parents. There was a moderate amount of agreement among the teacher and superintendent/school board leader groups, leading to the conclusion that the principals' planning processes are perceived to be, in descending order: (1) organizing, (2) providing for resources, (3) establishing needs, (4) recognizing the occasion for planning, (5) defining goals and objectives, (6) securing allegiances, (7) providing for needed training, and (8) providing for evaluation.

It is evident that curriculum planning involves several different individuals and groups, but that there is no one "typical" practice. Generally, there are two models: (1) "bottom up," from an individual or group through a department to the principal, through a committee, and to the central office for final approval; or (2) "top down," with an idea originating with an outside project or a university, getting central office support and the principal's approval. Funds often accompany the "top down" proposals.

The principal's role in curriculum varies considerably from school to school. A few principals indicated that they initiate ideas, often subtly through others, but more typically the principals view themselves as catalysts, facilitators, reviewers, and resource providers.

Principals list teachers, individually or by departments, as the primary initiators of curriculum changes, followed by building administrators and the central administration. Students and parents were mentioned infrequently. The schools tended to fall into the two previously noted categories, either "top down" or "bottom up."

Teachers overwhelmingly supported the "bottom up" view of curriculum change, with individual teachers in first place, followed by departments. All of the "significant others" groups also placed teachers and departments on top, but to a somewhat lesser extent. The superintendents/school board leaders tended to place the central office in a slighly more important role than did any of the other groups.

According to the principals, the major strength of their schools is the variety of offerings, which provides a comprehensive set of options for both the college-bound and the non-college-bound students. Another strength mentioned frequently is the quality of the teaching in the schools. Specific courses were cited in several instances.

All of the "significant others" agreed that the major strength of the school is the variety and diversity of the program. Offerings for the academically talented were the next most often mentioned strengths. Individualization and flexibility were also cited several times.

When specific programs or subjects were mentioned by "significant others," the vocational/technical fields were most frequently named. Science, math, English, business, and music were also mentioned frequently. Excellent teaching staffs were often cited by all the groups.

The major weaknesses, as seen by the principals of the 60 high schools, were more difficult to identify. Several fields and subjects were mentioned, but none by very many of the principals. The weakness stated most often was the lack of programs for low achievers and non-college-bound students.

Weaknesses as perceived by "significant others" tended to vary with the perspective of the group. Students tended to concentrate on weaknesses in subjects or programs for the college bound, presumably because the student leaders in the groups that were interviewed were college preparatory types. Teachers, parents, and superintendents/school board leaders were somewhat more concerned about weaknesses in vocational/technical offerings and programs for low achievers and the non-college-bound.

22

When asked how they anticipate curriculum needs and organize resources to meet such needs, principals mentioned a variety of methods. Frequently cited activities were informal discussions with staff and surveys of students' perceptions of need. Mandates by the state and the local board of education were also referred to frequently. A few principals stated that they get ideas from professional meetings and literature.

A typical process of achieving program change might be described as: (1) gaining awareness of need through mandates or requirements, surveys, and informal discussions; (2) formulating plans, usually through departments, with available staff and budget in mind; and (3) executing the change. Evaluation of the change was seldom mentioned.

As far as the development of extracurricular activities is concerned, the principals consider their role to be largely that of delegating, facilitating, and monitoring. Principals attend most of the activities such as games, concerts, and plays.

The principals' self-evaluations of their effectiveness in the area of curriculum development were placed on a five-point scale, from 1.0 (ineffective) to 5.0 (highly effective). The range was from 2.0 to 5.0, with a median of 4.0.

The "significant others" also rated the principals' effectiveness in curriculum development, on a five-point scale. Students and teachers gave median ratings of 4.0, which matched the principals' own median ratings. The superintendents/school board leaders gave a median rating of 4.5, and the parents' median was 5.0.

Program Evaluation

No clear pictures emerge from the principals' responses to the question: "How do you evaluate the outcomes of programs or projects initiated by you?" Evidently evaluation of programs is not high on the principals' list of priorities. Most of the principals admitted that little, if any, systematic evaluation is done, other than what is required by others.

When evaluation of programs does take place, the principals indicated that the central office, the teachers, and the high school administration are about equally involved. Students and parents were also mentioned by a few of the principals.

When asked *how* they provide for the evaluation of major events, projects, or programs, the principals often stated that they see to it that evaluation is built into the plans. Evidently the use of reactionnaires at the end of the process is the most common single method of evaluation. Informal evaluation seems to predominate over formal means. Only a small number of principals mentioned product measures.

The "significant others" groups were reluctant to express opinions about the principals' role in evaluation, because they had little or no knowledge of it. Those who did express opinions gave a wide variety of responses that revealed no clear patterns of behavior on the part of the principals. Perhaps the most significant aspect of this part of the study is the lack of awareness of the principals' role in such an important process as evaluation.

When asked to indicate how effective they regarded themselves to be in the area of program evaluation (with responses placed on a five-point scale, from 1.0, highly ineffective, to 5.0, highly effective), the principals' responses ranged from 2.0 to 5.0, with a median of 3.0. The "significant others" median ratings were all 4.0 except the parent leaders' median, which was 4.5; however, few of the students or parents made ratings at all.

4 The Nature of the Job

ACCORDING TO THE DATA gathered during interviews, slightly more than half of the principals have 11-month contracts; an additional third have 12-month contracts; and the remaining principals are employed for either 10 or 10½ months.

Almost two-thirds of the interviewees reported that they were working under one-year contracts; one-third indicated working under "continuous" contracts; three principals reported three-year contracts. If "continuous" means that the contract is automatically renewed from year to year, then only a minority of the principals have multiple-year contracts, such as are customary with superintendents.

An analysis of the principals' responses suggests that the typical principal's work day begins at 7:30 a.m. and ends around 5 p.m.—a total of 9½ hours. (The range extended from a 7½ hour day to a high of 15½ hours.) The data from the "significant others" indicate that they did not have a very clear idea of the principals' daily starting and quitting times. (This was particularly true of students and parents.) Surprisingly, however, the estimates of the "significant others" averaged out to a 9½ hour workday for the principal, which was the same average for the principals' responses.

The principals reported, on average, that they spent three nights a week on school business. This included attendance at board meetings, athletic and other extracurricular events, and various meetings at the school. Half of the principals indicated that they worked weekends on a variety of tasks, especially supervising activities, "catching-up," and planning for the week ahead or for a special activity. Interestingly, a number of principals indicated that they deliberately try to avoid weekend work if at all possible.

The "significant others" cited an extremely wide range of activities that they thought occupied a great deal of the principals' time out-

25

William Kritek, assistant professor of education at the University of Wisconsin—Milwaukee, contributed to the initial development of parts of this chapter and chapter five.

side regular school hours. These activities ranged from attendance at school board meetings and meetings with parents to attendance at athletic and other events. Also cited were involvement with community agencies and service clubs, attendance at professional meetings, etc.

Table 1 provides data on the principals' *planned* time and the time *actually* spent in a number of task areas over a two-week period prior to the interviews. Column one ranks the areas in terms of time *scheduled* for those two weeks. Column two ranks the areas in terms of time *actually* spent. The numbers in these columns, as well as the numbers in the other tables in this chapter, are mean rankings for the interview responses; the number one represents the most time and the number nine the least time.

The data in Table 1 indicate that the principals actually spent their time during the two weeks prior to the interviews in a manner that closely approximated their scheduled use of that time. In four of the nine areas the principals spent, on the average, the same relative proportion of time as they had scheduled for themselves. Student behavior, school management, and personnel took more of the principals' time than they had scheduled. On the other hand, the principals were not able to spend as much time as they would have liked in the areas of planning and program development, particularly the latter.

TABLE 1
Principals' Planned Time and Time Spent

Area of Activity	Time Planned (Biweekly)	Time Spent (Biweekly)
Program Development (curriculum, instructional leadership)	1	3
Personnel (evaluation, advising, conferencing, recruiting)	2	1
School Management (weekly calendar, office, budget, correspondence, memos, etc.)	3	2
Student Activities (meetings, supervision, planning)	4	4
District Office (meetings, task forces, reports, etc.)	5	5
Community (PTA, advisory groups, parent conferences)	6	6
Planning (annual, long-range)	7	9
Professional Development (reading, conferences, etc.)	8	8
Student Behavior (discipline, attendance, meetings)	9	7

Factors That Influence How the Principals Spent Their Time

As a follow-up to Table 1, the principals were asked a number of questions about what factors influenced how they spent their time.

Virtually all the principals reported that what they did on a given day was determined, at least in part, by advance planning. Also, the weekly agenda of assigned responsibilities played a major role. Despite advance planning and assigned responsibilities, the principals indicated that what a principal does each day is also influenced by events that "just come up."

An examination of principals' responses concerning planning the use of time suggests that this planning process is highly idiosyncratic, varying greatly from individual to individual. Some principals rely on yearly or monthly calendars of activities; some are helped by weekly bulletins prepared for staff; some maintain a "things to do" list. The majority indicated that they spent some time at the end of the week planning for the next week. This is usually done late Friday afternoon or at home over the weekend. Finally, important decisions on the use of the time are made in various meetings—the administrative team, department, task force, etc.

When asked what kinds of interruptions kept them from adhering to their planned use of time, the principals identified "crises," "emergencies in the building," and "discipline problems" as typical interruptions. Another frequently cited interruption is intrusions by telephone or drop-in visitors. A number of the principals indicated that they felt their job required an open-door policy—and the interruptions that are associated with it. (Apparently the "significant others" felt that, in general, the principals had an open-door policy, as they gave very high ratings on a five-point accessibility scale. Parents rated the principal the highest, 4.8 mean rating; followed by teachers 4.6; central office/school board 4.5; and students 4.1.)

The principals were also asked whether or not they felt that they wasted any time and, if so, to describe the circumstances. About a fourth of them did not feel they wasted any time. A number of other principals commented that time which some people might see as wasted, such as walking around the building and neighborhood, was not in fact wasted.

By far the most frequently cited "time-waster" was attending meetings. District office meetings were listed most frequently by the principals as the biggest waste of time. Two other factors frequently cited by principals as time-wasters were: (1) too much paper work, and (2) problems referred to the principal which could or should have been handled by some other person in the school. However, these factors were mentioned much less frequently as time wasters than the various meetings the principals were required to attend. In fact, in examining all the data, one receives the impression that if the required district office meetings could be improved or eliminated, many principals' time problems could be greatly ameliorated.

When asked what suggestions they would give to other principals for coping with the problem of insufficient time, the effective principals have a wide variety of responses. However, the basic elements of their recommendations were the following:

- Don't get up-tight if you don't get everything done that you set out to do. There will be another day.

27

- Don't get bogged down in paperwork. Delegate, use time management.

- Set priorities, but be flexible in case priorities change.

- Delegate responsibility. A principal can't do everything.

- Monitor delegated responsibility and set high expectations for accomplishment.

- Be better organized. Do advance and long-range planning so you aren't caught by surprise. Outline plans on a weekly, monthly, and yearly basis.

Yearly Time Allocations and Priorities

An attempt was made to ascertain how the principals spent their time on a yearly basis, as well as how they thought they *should* be spending their time. These data are reported in Table 2. In column one the areas of activity are ranked according to the amount of time spent in each area during the work year. Column two ranks the areas according to how the principals felt they *should* spend their time during the course of a year.

TABLE 2
Principals' Time Allocations and Priorities

Area of Activity	Time Spent (Year)	Should Spend (Year)
School Management (weekly calendar, office, budget, correspondence, memos, etc.)	1	3
Personnel (evaluation, advising, conferencing, recruiting)	2	1
Program Development (curriculum, instructional leadership)	3	2
Student Activities (meetings, supervision, planning)	4	4
Student Behavior (discipline, attendance, meetings)	5	8
Planning (annual, long-range)	6	5
Community (PTA, advisory groups, parent conferences)	7	6
District Office (meetings, task forces, reports, etc.)	8	7
Professional Development (reading, conferences, etc.)	9	9

Columns one and two show for the most part general agreement between how the principals would like to spend their time and how they actually spent it over the course of a year. The only two major exceptions appear to be in the areas of school management and student behavior. In both cases, particularly the latter, the principals spent more time than they think they should be investing in these activities.

Although the principals reported that they would like to spend the most time on personnel, followed by program development, they actually spent the most time on school management, which they agreed should have a lower priority than the other two areas. The principals indicated that they should spend the next-to-least amount of time during the year on student behavior, but in reality they spent more time on this area than on planning, community, district office, or professional development.

Worth noting is that the area the principals felt should have the *lowest* priority for their time was professional development, which also perfectly reflected their time allocation to this area. The low priority on time allocation given to community and district office is also noteworthy.

Since the areas of school management and student behavior took more time than many principals desired, an attempt was made to analyze the responses of those principals who indicated that they spent more time on either of these tasks than they thought desirable. The analysis revealed that the following factors were influencing these principals:

- lack of administrative staff
- the need to be visible to students
- emergencies, crisis management
- discipline problems
- immediate ongoing needs of people
- administrivia, the paper bureaucracy.

Similarly, an analysis of responses given by principals who indicated they spent time in these categories exactly as they thought appropriate revealed the following conditions:

- very capable assistant principals
- faith in others to perform assigned responsibilities
- ability to delegate
- ability to operate according to priority goals.

In general, what factors determine how a principal spends his time over the course of a year? In response to this question, the principals tended not to cite short- or long-range planning factors, indicating instead that they were at the mercy of others. For example, federal and state regulations and district office requirements necessitated extensive paper work, forms to be completed, and reports to be submitted.

Also, the principals frequently mentioned that they needed to respond to the needs of staff and students, and the importance of symbolic leadership was emphasized. Finally, some principals noted that they allocated their time according to personal and professional interests. However, it would appear that the way the principal spends his time during the year is influenced more by the needs and expectations of others than by the principal's own vision, long-range planning, and priorities.

Significant Others' Perceptions and Expectations

The "significant others" were asked for their perceptions of how the principals spent their time and how they should be spending their time. Table 3 presents data from the responses to these questions. The "Per." columns present the significant others' perceptions of how the principals spend their time; the "Prio." columns present the "significant others'" priorities as to how the principals *ought* to spend their time.

TABLE 3
Significant Others' Time Perceptions and Priorities
Compared to Principals

Principals' Time Spent and Time Priorities *	Teachers'		Central Office		Parents		Students	
	Per.**	Prio.***	Per.	Prio.	Per.	Prio.	Per.	Prio.
1. Personnel (1)	2	2	1	2	2	2	3	4
2. Management (3)	1	3	2	3	1	1	1	2
3. Program Development (2)	5	1	3	1	3	3	2	1
4. Student Activities (4)	4	4	4	4	4	4	4	3
5. District Office (7)	3	9	8	8	5	9	5	9
6. Community (6)	8	7	5	6	8	7	8	5
7. Student Behavior (8)	6	6	7	7	7	6	7	6
8. Professional Development (9)	9	8	9	9	9	8	9	8
9. Planning (5)	7	5	6	5	6	5	6	7

*   The task areas are listed in the order in which the principals actually spent their time over a two-week period of time. The ranks in parentheses indicate how the principals felt they should be spending their time over the period of a year.

** Perceptions (do)

***Priorities (should)

Table 3 indicates that the four groups of "significant others," with some exceptions, were generally in agreement regarding their perceptions of how the principals actually spend their time. What the table does not show is that the "significant others" were apparently *not very knowledgeable* about how the principals spend their time. This conclusion is based on the fact that less than one-third of the parents and only about half of the central office/school board, teacher, and student groups could or would estimate how the principals spend their time. Few of the referent groups' interviewees could speak with any certainty regarding this question. This must be kept in mind in interpreting the "significant others" findings.

When the perceptions of the "significant others" regarding how the principals spend their time are compared with how the principals *actually* spend their time, a fairly high degree of congruence is evident.

However, there are several noteworthy exceptions. For example, all the "significant others" believed that the principals spend proportionately *more* time on planning, professional development, and (with the exception of the central office/school board) on school management than the principals report that they do. On the other hand, with the exception of the central office/school board, the "significant others" believed that the principals spend *less* time on personnel and community than the principals reported they do.

Turning to the priority columns, Table 3 shows a fairly high level of agreement, but it has shown some discrepancies between the priorities of the "significant others" and their perceptions of how the principals spend their time. For example, teachers placed top priority on program development but believed the principal allocated time in such a manner that program development was relegated to fifth place (out of the possible nine places).

All the "significant others" groups placed a very low priority on spending time on district office meetings, reports, task forces, etc. However, teachers, parents, and students perceived the principal as devoting relatively more time to district office matters than they thought desirable. The teachers, in fact, perceived the principal as allocating so much time to the district office that it ranked third. (They would have preferred that it rank ninth.) At the same time, the superintendent and board members did not think the principal was allocating too much time to the district office—their perception of time spent is identical to the priority they place on that use of time.

Despite these discrepancies, however, the priorities of the "significant others," with few exceptions, are in relatively high agreement with the priorities of the principals as to how they should spend their time. Therefore, it appears that the effective principal operates in a situation in which the expectations of others are reasonably congruent with his own priorities.

Conditions of the Job

The principals were asked to identify three aspects of the job situation which enabled them to be effective as principals and three significant constraints which made the job more difficult than it should be.

Those factors identified most frequently as contributing to the principal's effectiveness had to do with support given the principal:

- quality and support of the faculty
- central office support and trust
- cooperative students, "good kids"
- parental and community support and cooperation.

Other factors were cited less frequently, but were also judged to be important. Generally, these factors also related to support:

- autonomy of the principal, no interference from central office
- competent administrative staff
- competent secretary
- good financial support, adequate resources
- high status given the principalship.

In addition, a number of personal qualities were mentioned by the principals as helping them to be effective. These included an interest in and liking for the job, the capacity to work long hours, confidence in others, and the ability to delegate.

The "significant others" groups were also requested to identify conditions of the job which they felt were especially helpful to the principal. The factor perceived by students, teachers, and parents to be most helpful to the principal was a supportive staff; for the central office group, it was the existence of a supportive central office.

Adequate assistance was the condition next most frequently cited by students, teachers, and the central office as being helpful to the principal, while parents identified the presence of a supportive community. "Supportive students" was the third most helpful condition identified by the students themselves and the teachers, but the parents and the central office generally gave this factor a relatively low ranking. Also, the presence of a supportive community was given much less emphasis by students, teachers, and the central office groups than the other factors previously discussed.

Interestingly, the "significant others" generally did not believe that the existence of an affluent school district was a very helpful condition to the principal. This can be explained, at least in part, by the fact that many of the "significant others" felt that the principal operated in a situation of limited funds.

Regarding important constraints or conditions of the job that make it more difficult than it should be, a number of factors were identified by the principals. Cited most frequently were:

- limited or inadequate resources, budget restrictions
- too much paper work
- lack of administrative assistance.

Another constraining factor mentioned somewhat less frequently was "interruptions in work schedule." The sources of these interruptions were the central office, community, staff, parents, or students. Included under this heading were parents' inclinations to deal only with the principal, helping faculty solve personal problems, unrealistic requests by school board members, and dealing with student discipline problems. Such interruptions were perceived by a number of principals to place demands on their time, causing them to be less productive.

Finally, there was another group of constraining factors which, although mentioned less frequently than the other conditions, made the job more difficult in the eyes of the principals. These factors were:

- the teachers' union contract, collective bargaining
- inadequate facilities
- court decisions that tie the hands of school people
- lack of central office support
- general feeling of the public toward public education.

The "significant others," when asked to identify conditions of the job that might make it difficult for the principal, tended to cite far fewer difficult factors than helpful ones. In fact, an analysis of the data revealed no commonly perceived constraint by any of the "significant others" groups.

Several minority trends were identified, however. For example, parents most frequently cited an apathetic or critical community as a difficult condition for the principal, with a smaller number focusing on an interfering or nonsupportive school board. The central office and/or school board was also most often mentioned by teachers as a constraint upon the principal's effectiveness, followed by limited financial resources.

Students most often mentioned the community as representing a problem for the principal but, surprisingly, reported next in frequency as contributing to the principal's difficulties were nonsupportive students.

The central office group agreed most frequently with parents and students that the principal's greatest constraint was posed by an apathetic or nonsupportive community. The next most frequently mentioned problem was nonsupportive students, followed by inflexible or overcrowded facilities. The views of parents and teachers to the contrary, central office personnel identified themselves as the least difficult group with which the principal had to work.

When one examines all the factors, both positive and negative, it would appear that there are some common elements. Supportive and cooperative people seem to be the key to facilitating the principals' effectiveness; inadequate resources and pressures on the principals' time seem to hinder the principal the most. Both factors are probably not peculiar to effective principals and may be generic to the job of principal.

A final question in the job section of the effective principals' interview asked them to indicate whether or not in their district the principals negotiated with the central office on working conditions and salary, and if so, what role in the negotiations they played. Half the principals in the study stated that in their districts they did negotiate formally with the central office on salary and working conditions, and that they most typically did this as part of a school administrators' association or group.

Many of the remaining principals, excluding those in parochial schools, appeared to have some informal kinds of negotiating going on, but no formal bargaining. In general, it appears that the effective high school principal is more likely than not to be in a district which either already has collective bargaining for middle management or seems to be moving in that direction.

5 Solving Problems and Causing Change

PRINCIPALS WERE ASKED TO IDENTIFY a difficult problem that they had handled well and one they had not handled as well, and to describe the process employed in addressing each. They were also asked to rate their problem-solving effectiveness on a five-point scale.

The vast majority of the principals saw themselves as effective problem solvers, with most rating themselves as four or five, which was high on the five-point scale used. They also tended to report more frequently problems that they felt they had handled well than problems which they believed they had not handled well. An analysis of the types of problems identified by the principals revealed several major categories.

The most frequently cited category of problems that principals felt they had handled well dealt with student misbehavior, particularly discipline problems, and problems in the extracurricular program. The category of problems most frequently mentioned as not being handled well was *teacher behavior,* for example, teacher incompetency. It must be emphasized, however, that in individual cases student misbehavior was reported as a problem handled poorly and teacher behavior handled well.

In order to obtain data from several perspectives on the types of problems principals handled, the principals' "significant others" were also asked to identify a problem that they thought the principal had handled well and one which they believed he had not handled as well. For the most part, there was little agreement at the individual school level among the four reference groups and with the principals on which specific problems they had handled well or poorly. However, in regard to problems the principals handled well, students and parents tended to report problems involving the extracurricular program most frequently, while teachers cited student behavior problems, and the central office mentioned parent/community problems.

In general, the "significant others" had more difficulty in identifying a problem that the principal did not handle well. In fact, in a large number of schools, two or more of the "significant others" could not think of a single problem that the principal did not handle well. Perhaps surprisingly, the kinds of problems that the principal did not handle well were *not* dissimilar in type to the kinds they said the principal handled well. As a group, students tended more frequently to report problems that the principal did not handle well, followed by teachers, central office staff, and then parents.

It is worthwhile noting at this point the kinds of problems that principals and the significant others did *not* report with any high degree of frequency in identifying problems handled well or not so well.

For example, problems involving the curriculum were seldom reported. Problems relating to supervision of instruction were also seldom mentioned. School-community problems were noted more frequently, but not nearly as often as problems involving students or teachers. This suggests that the principal for the most part is either not addressing problems in these areas or people are unaware of such efforts.

An examination of the problem-solving *approach* described by the principals in dealing with a problem they handled well and one which they didn't handle well revealed several interesting findings.

In regard to dealing with a problem they handled well, the principals seemed to employ one of three approaches, although some principals utilized more than one approach.

One group of principals tended to utilize principles and steps of problem solving and to employ a *process* of problem solving recommended in the professional literature. These principals, when confronted with a problem:

1. *Investigated* and *diagnosed* the factors which seemed to be the cause of the problem.

2. *Identified* and *assessed* the various alternative means of resolving the problem; looked creatively for that third or fourth or fifth alternative.

3. *Met* with a variety of people, particularly those who were to be affected by the problem or its resolution.

4. Utilized *mediation, counter proposals,* and *compromise* in their approach to problem solving.

5. Selected a proposed resolution of the problem only *after considerable analysis and thought.*

6. Planned carefully and thoughtfully the *implementation* of the proposed solution.

A second group of principals, smaller in number, emphasized the importance of the personal qualities of the problem solver when they solved problems. The personal characteristics they felt to be most important were:

- being a good listener
- not becoming defensive or emotional
- being able to take pressure or tension
- staying cool
- being fair and reasonable, but firm
- showing stick-to-it-iveness.

A third group of principals, the largest in number, appeared to use an intuitive approach in problem solving. In analyzing the approach employed by these principals, it was difficult to ascertain a definable process or set of personal characteristics, but the holding of meetings seemed to be the predominant technique utilized. This group of principals seemingly had no more difficulty solving problems than the other two groups of principals, but they were more intuitive in their approach or less detailed in describing it.

While the principals' descriptions of the approaches they applied to problems they felt they *did not* handle well were often lacking in detail, a number of instructive points were made. The following quotations best illustrate the types of mistakes:

- "I sort of waited, hoping the problem would resolve itself, but it didn't."
- "I acted impulsively and hastily."
- "I reacted too quickly without fully understanding the nature of the problem."
- "I tended to let the problem affect my emotions and I overreacted."
- "I didn't weigh all the alternatives and implications."
- "I didn't consider carefully enough the consequences and the implications."
- "I didn't involve sufficiently the people who would be affected by the proposed resolution of the problem."

It would appear that emotions and the lack of a problem-solving process are two major factors that contribute to reduced effectiveness in those situations the principals felt they did not handle well.

In addition to requesting principals to describe the problem-solving approaches they actually used, they were also asked to identify what they believed to be the most important components of problem solving, and the factors which influenced them in determining when to make a decision. Although the responses to these questions were diverse, the components of problem solving identified were quite similar to the process and personal qualities cited by the first two groups of principals when asked to describe the approach they employed in dealing with a problem they handled well. In identifying the important components of problem solving, however, most of the principals appeared to be more analytical and descriptive in their comments than in reporting the actual approach they employed in solving problems.

An analysis of the principals' responses to the question of what factors influence a principal in determining when to make a decision suggests that this depends on the complexity of the problem, the need for more investigation and information, the amount of involvement by others needed, and the need to develop acceptance of the proposed decision. In general, the principals seemed to feel that much depends on the nature of the situation necessitating a decision, but that it is important neither to procrastinate nor to rush.

When one examines the data on the "significant others" descriptions of the problem-solving approach employed by the principal, several interesting dimensions emerge. First of all, although there were some exceptions, the "significant others" did not appear to be knowledgeable about the approach or process the principal utilized in solving a problem, other than being aware that he called a meeting or scheduled a conference. Secondly, the "significant others" really didn't seem to be too concerned about the approach or problem solving process the principal employed as long as he resolved the problem successfully. When the "significant others" did discuss what the principal did to solve the problem, they tended to emphasize the personal qualities of the principal rather than any process of problem solving.

Finally, the evidence the "significant others" used as a basis for judging whether or not a problem had been successfully resolved appeared skimpy at best, and lacked reliability and validity. The main criterion which the "significant others" seemed to be employing as to whether or not a problem had been successfully resolved was the degree to which the resolution met *their* expectations, which may or may not have been the expectations of the participants associated with the problem. For the most part, the students and parents tended to judge the principal's effectiveness as a problem solver on whether or not he acted fairly and decisively about the student problem, involving them when appropriate.

For teachers, the criterion for effectiveness was whether or not the principal was firm in disciplining students and supported teachers in a conflict with a student and parent, and for the central office it tended to be whether or not the principal acted prudently and according to school district policy. Regardless of the nature of their expectations, however, the "significant others" by and large rated the principal as an effective problem solver. Parents tended to give the highest effectiveness rating to the principal, followed by students, central office, and then teachers.

The responses of the "significant others" on the role of the principal as a problem solver strongly suggest that it is the nature of the outcome, not the process of problem solving, which is of the most concern to the "significant others," and that the outcome must meet their particular expectation for success, not some more generalizable or objective standard of effectiveness.

The Principal as Change Agent

In recent years there have been a number of studies and publications calling for the reform of secondary school education in the United States. These studies and publications offer the principal one good source of ideas for needed changes in the school. Therefore, the principals in the study were asked whether or not they were acquainted with each of the following reports and the extent to which they had been useful:

The Reform of Secondary Education, Report of National Commission.

Vitalizing the High School, Association for Supervision and Curriculum Development.

Youth: Transition to Adulthood, President's Panel on Youth.

New Roles for Youth in the School and Community, Report of National Commission on Resources for Youth.

The Education of Adolescents, Report of National Panel on High Schools.

Rise, Report of the California Commission for Reform of Intermediate and Secondary Education.

The Adolescent, Other Citizens, and Their High Schools, Task Force '74.

Secondary Schools in a Changing Society: This We Believe, NASSP Task Force.

The Boundless Resource: A Prospectus for an Education/Work Policy, National Manpower Institute.

Slightly more than half the principals reported that they were acquainted with the NASSP Task Force Report, *Secondary Schools in a Changing Society: This We Believe.* Also, one-half of the principals knew of the National Commission's report, *The Reform of Secondary Education.* Much smaller numbers of principals were acquainted with any of the other recent national reports on the reform of secondary education.

Although the data are not precise, it appears that a sizable percentage of the principals indicated no knowledge of any of the other reports identified in the interview. In addition, while some of the principals circulated the reports, referred to them at faculty meetings, or used them in an inservice program, it seems that the impact on school programs has been minimal. Four principals did indicate that the reports led to a program of credit for out-of-school learning activities or for a program aimed at bringing the community into the school.

When asked what major changes had occurred during the past year or two in their schools in which they had played a major role, the principals indicated a range of innovations, from school climate to alterations in the physical plant. However, changes in the curriculum were cited twice as often as any other type of change. Tied for second place in the number of citations were changes in student behavior, changes in management procedures, and changes in school climate. As implied above, each of these types of change was mentioned approximately half as frequently as curricular change.

The "significant others," in responding to a similar question about major changes in the school in which the principal had played a major role, agreed for the most part with the principals on the types of changes which had occurred. However, the "significant others" tended to perceive many *fewer* changes in which the principal had played a major role than did the principals themselves. For example, the parents identified approximately 72 percent fewer changes in which the principals had played a major role than did the principals. In the case of the students and the teachers, they cited approximately 52 percent fewer changes than did the principals, while the central office identified 46 percent fewer changes. The same pattern of "significant others" identifying fewer changes also prevailed in comparing responses on specific types of change.

In considering the perceptions of the "significant others" as to specific types of changes occurring in the school in which the principals played a major role, the area of curricular change (although mentioned less than half as frequently as it was by the principals) was identified most frequently by teachers, the central office, and parents, while curricular change was the third most frequently cited area by students. Students reported school climate most frequently as a change area, followed by student behavior. Community relations was cited *least* frequently as a major change area by students and teachers and next to last in frequency by parents. The central office identified the area of student activities as the area of least change in the school in which the principal had played a major role.

According to the principals, the idea for the major changes most often originated from the principal himself. The principals also saw themselves as the "initiators" or "facilitators" of major changes in the school, but seldom reported that they engaged in the role as planners, consultants, or evaluators of change.

All the "significant others" agreed with the principals that in situations where there had been a major change in the school, with the principal playing a major role, the most typical originator of the idea had been the principal. However, the "significant others" perceived the principal as the originator of the idea for change less frequently than did the principals themselves. The parents, for example, saw the principal as the originator of the idea for change only about one-third as often as did the principals, while the students and the teachers identified the principal as the originator of the idea for change two-thirds as often as did the principals. The central office for the most part agreed with the principals on who originated the idea for change.

The "significant others" agreed with the principals that in regard to changes in which the principal had played a major role, the principal's role in the change process was that of initiator or facilitator, although students, teachers, and parents saw the principal in these roles less frequently than did the principals. In a majority of schools the "significant others" did not observe the principal in the role of planner, consultant, or evaluator in the change process.

The faculty, occasionally in consort with the community or parents or some other group, was perceived by the principals as the main source of resistance to major change in the school. However, in approximately one-third of the cited examples, the principals reported no resistance to the attempted change.

Virtually every principal indicated that he had a particular strategy that was typically used to bring about change. These strategies varied considerably, both in content and in the degree to which they were articulated. A composite change strategy, however, would contain the following three elements—listed according to the frequency with which they were mentioned:

- Work with people—especially those who will be affected. Get them involved and keep them involved. Do not impose change on people. Solicit their advice and input.

- Recognize the need for change and plant the seed or raise the ideas with staff and others.

- Provide needed resources and get the support of significant individuals or groups.

41

Also mentioned (but infrequently) were elements that may be described as "plan carefully" and "promote an atmosphere in which others can develop proposals for and attempts at change."

The principals were also asked to identify an imposed change, its source, and the principal's response. The imposed changes cited ran the gamut from staff reduction and a new attendance policy imposed by a school board to state and federal statutes regarding Title IX, the 18-

year-old as adult law, students with exceptional educational needs, and desegregation. The tone of the principals' responses suggested resentment and anger over the imposition, coupled with an attempt at coping. In addition, the principals complained about poor planning on the part of the outside agency or organization prior to the implementation of the change.

Since effective leadership is needed to introduce change successfully, the principals were asked, "What do you think constitutes good leadership?" This question generated a wide variety of responses, but those cited in order of frequency were the following:

- Working with others, getting things done through others.
- Having respect for and consideration of people: honesty, fairness, consistency, responsive to others' needs, sharing the credit for success, having confidence in people.
- Having a willingness to work hard and set high standards.
- Being decisive, willing to take a risk, having strong convictions.

Apparently, whatever change strategy and leadership qualities the principals employed, they were generally effective, according to the "significant others." When asked to evaluate the principal's role as a change agent on a five-point scale on which five was high, the students gave the principal the highest rating, 4.7; followed by the parents with 4.6; the teachers with 4.4; and the central office with 4.2.

42

6 Professional Views and Assessments

ALL THE PRINCIPALS WERE ASKED if they knew why they were selected for their present position, how long they intended to remain in that position, and what their long-range plans were.

The most frequent response given to the question of why the principals were selected for their current position was that they had been an assistant or vice principal in the same school and had performed well in that job. The next most frequent response was that ability to innovate and bring about needed changes was an important consideration, and in certain situations it apparently helped to be a female or a member of a minority group.

The remainder of the responses from the principals did not show a pattern but ranged from "Guess I was just good" to "Came in the back door when six others battled and eliminated themselves." Worth noting is that in many cases the principals seemed not to be very knowledgeable about why they were selected or they were reluctant to discuss the reasons.

An examination of the data on the same question from the "significant others" revealed that the most frequent response for the students and the parents was that they didn't know why the principal was selected for the job. At a number of schools the teachers also did not appear to know why the principal had been selected. The most common reason given by any of the "significant others," including the central office/school board group, was that the principal was selected because of his previous administrative experience, for example, a vice principal in the same school; and educational baclground. Individual comments by "significant others" which suggested qualities of the principal beyond experience and background were:

- "He has always been outstanding in everything he has done."
- "Experienced in innovative education."
- "Compassionate—always concerned with individual students."
- "The fact that he was young, black, and extremely competent made him a logical choice."

43

- "The school had a bad reputation and he was strong and capable of turning the situation around."

When the principals were asked how long they intended to remain as principal of the school, the most frequent response given was "only a year or two"; the next most frequent response was that they already had another job lined up for next year. Although some principals indicated that they planned to stay in their present jobs for a long period of time, the responses of most principals suggest that the effective high school principal is not planning to stay very long in the present position and that he is upwardly mobile.

While the long-range plans of the principals appeared somewhat diverse, ranging from university teaching to another principalship, the most common response seemed to envision some type of move to a central office position, with the superintendency mentioned most frequently.

Concerns and Constraints

In response to a question about the things that tended to bother them, the principals most frequently cited incompetent and uncommitted teachers. For example, teachers who were not prepared, who were unwilling to take responsibility outside the classroom, and who were not willing to give 100 percent bothered the principals. Also, teachers who wanted to work only with students who were self-motivated and cooperative were of concern to a number of principals.

The other aspects listed by more than one principal as bothering them were diverse, but included such items as too many unnecessary district meetings; unprofessional teacher conduct such as gossiping and bickering; student misbehavior; student dropouts; unfair parent, teacher, and board expectations; and inadequate funds and facilities.

From the viewpoint of the "significant others," a number of things tended to bother the principal and cause him worry or stress. Students seemed to feel that student misbehavior, particularly vandalism, bothered the principal the most, followed by bad public relations and parent and school board interference. Parents also felt that student misbehavior was of most concern to the principal, followed by critics who run down the school, and parental apathy.

Teachers and the central office indicated they felt that uncommitted teachers and those who didn't produce were of most concern to the principal. Interestingly, the second most frequently cited factor mentioned by the central office as bothering the principal was central office interference or nonsupport.

In regard to the main institutional (school) and social (society) constraints that may handicap the principal in doing a good job, there was fairly high agreement between the principal and the "significant others" groups.

The constraints identified most frequently by the principals were the physical limitations of the building they were in, the limited budget under which they worked, and community pressures and interferences. Other factors listed less frequently included the district master contract, federal mandates of one kind or another, lack of administrative help, and a deluge of paper work.

The teachers, parents, and central office groups tended to agree with the principal on the most important constraint in that they also cited most frequently the limitations of the budget. In the case of the students, they were more likely to see the attitude of the community as the most important constraint.

However, the second most frequent constraint they mentioned was finances, along with the restrictions of the central office and the school board, while the central office/school board groups mentioned the limitations of the facilities. Other factors identified less frequently as constraints on the principal were value conflicts which were mentioned by the central office and court decisions which were mentioned by the teachers.

In general, it appears that a limited budget, an inadequate building, a restrictive central office and/or school board, and interfering parents were the main constraints that hampered the principal. It also seems clear that while institutional and social constraints overlap, the constraints identified most frequently seemed to be more institutional than social in nature.

As far as the future is concerned, the "significant others" believe that several major school conditions or societal forces are likely to have a significant influence upon the school during the next three to five years. The three most important, according to all of the "significant others," are: (1) enrollment changes; (2) the general state of the economy, and the local financial situation; and, (3) the demand for basics.

The demand for basics was mentioned as the third most likely influence by students, parents, and the central office, while teachers saw it as the second most likely influence. All the "significant others" agreed that enrollment changes were most likely to have an important influence on the school in the next three to five years. Surprisingly, student competency testing, staff competency, and compulsory education, for the most part, were not mentioned very often as possible influences.

Stress

In answer to the question, "How do you deal with stress?" the principals gave a variety of responses. Interestingly, almost a sixth of the principals said that stress was not a problem in their jobs. Also, while a small number of principals indicated that they didn't handle stress very well, the impression received from the interviews and from

45

examining the principals' responses was that, for the majority of the principals in this sample, stress was either not a major problem in their jobs or they had developed techniques for minimizing its potentially deleterious effects.

The techniques which the principals had evolved to handle stress appeared to fall into four major categories. The most frequent was to get away from the conditions provoking the stress. This took two forms: (1) getting out of the office or away from wherever the stress was being felt and walking around the building or school grounds, and (2) engaging in some type of recreational activity after work.

Examples of recreational activities employed by principals to relieve stress were obvious things like golf, bowling, tennis, racquet ball, and jogging. However, some not-so-obvious activities were reading and writing poetry, wood carving, glass staining, and meditation. It appeared that the principals were fairly individualistic in the type of recreational activity they selected to relieve their stress and no one single recreational activity, with the exception perhaps of jogging, stood out.

A second major approach utilized by principals to handle stress was to develop a sense of perspective about the problem of stress. This perspective seemed to contain the following elements:

> Stress is associated with the job. Try not to let it get to you or overwhelm you. Be realistic about what can be accomplished. Do your best and don't worry about it. Regardless of how bad things seem to be, there will always be a tomorrow. Keep a sense of humor about yourself and the job.

The principals who appeared to have a sense of perspective in dealing with stress also frequently utilized other techniques such as recreation, but a sense of perspective seemed to be the major tool they employed for handling stress.

A third approach a number of principals used in handling stress was to discuss the stress with others, including professional colleagues, such as the assistant principal, the superintendent, or the principal's spouse. However, it should be noted that this approach was not often turned to by the principal. Whether this means that principals believe that the stress they experience should not be discussed with others because it might reflect poorly on them or because they don't want to bother other people about their problems is not known. It is possible that principals do not feel that others would understand their situations. In any regard, not many principals employed this frequently recommended way of relieving stress.

This conclusion is supported by the finding that when the principals were asked, "With whom do you find it helpful and rewarding to share your professional problems?" a majority of them said, "No one," or didn't give a response. The overwhelming impression gained from examining the data on how the principals handled stress

46

and the extent to which they shared problems with others is that the principalship is a lonely position with few opportunities to relieve stress by discussing problems with people who might be helpful.

A fourth way that some principals indicated that they dealt with stress was to diagnose the causes of the stress and attempt to modify those causes. However, not many principals employed this approach. For the most part, the responses to the question of handling stress suggest that the majority of principals lack techniques for dealing directly with or removing the conditions causing their job stress. On the other hand, perhaps most principals felt that there was little they could do about the stress that they felt in their jobs and that the best way to handle the stress was to get away from it in hopes that the situation would improve.

Strengths and Limitations

An attempt was made during the interviews to ascertain the strengths and limitations of the principals, both from their perceptions and the perceptions of the "significant others."

As far as the principals were concerned, a majority felt that their strongest asset was their ability to relate well to different kinds of people:

- "People trust me, feel I'm honest."
- "I have insight into people, especially children."
- "I am able to make people feel at ease in any contact they have with me."

As a result of their ability to relate well to people, the principals felt that they were able to get the best out of people and were able to persuade them to follow their leadership.

Many principals also indicated that they were strong in communication and administrative skills, which includes the abilities to explain changes, sell ideas, and organize activities. The "significant others" tended to see the principal as stronger in oral communication than in written expression, and more effective in one-on-one situations than in group settings.

In addition, a number of principals felt that their strong commitment to quality education and their willingness and capacity to work hard and long hours were major strengths. Much less frequently cited, but still mentioned by a few principals as strengths, were their knowledge of the curriculum and their instructional improvement skills. Seldom mentioned as a strength was school-community relations, long-range planning, program evaluation, or student discipline. Interestingly, these areas were not identified by the principals as limitations either.

47

When the "significant others" were asked what they perceived as the principal's strengths, the most frequent response by students, parents, and teachers was the principal's ability to relate well to people, particularly students. The central office felt that the principal's strongest asset was his personality, in terms of being flexible, open, fair, candid, confident, and dedicated. The student, teacher, and parent groups also mentioned many of these same characteristics in discussing the principal's strengths. In general, the "significant others" saw the strengths of the principal much as he did, and in terms of personal characteristics rather than professional expertise.

An examination of the principals' responses to the question of what they considered to be their main limitations in handling their job revealed no majority trend as to *specific* weaknesses. However, in general, the principals tended to identify fewer weaknesses than strengths (which perhaps is not surprising when one considers that they had been selected as exemplary principals) and they were less detailed in discussing their weaknesses as compared to their strengths.

While some principals appeared quite open and insightful in discussing their limitations, others seemed to have difficulty in responding to the question. An example of the latter is suggested by the fact that the most common limitation cited by the principals was not a personal or professional weakness, but a limitation of the situation itself, such as a restrictive budget, or undedicated teachers, or too much paper work.

Also, a number of principals indicated that they didn't feel that they possessed any limitations, which may be true or may reflect a certain lack of insight. However, it should be remembered that the sample of principals selected for the study had been identified as exemplary and therefore might be expected to possess few weaknesses.

As far as specific weaknesses are concerned—although there was no majority trend in the data—those most frequently cited by principals tended to fall into the following three categories in order of frequency:

A. *Personality Characteristics:* too authoritarian, come on too strongly, too easy going, get angry too easily, impatient with people—impatient with the status quo, act impulsively, tend to be a perfectionist, too emotional, don't think enough before speaking, not as open as I would like, not as articulate as I should be, should be more tolerant when people differ with me.

B. *Deficient Organizational Skills:* spread myself too thin, don't use time effectively enough, not organized as well as I would like to be, need to delegate more, need to prioritize better, need to do more long-range planning.

C. *Limited Professional Development:* don't do as much professional reading as I should, need to take more course work, need to keep up better with national trends and what is going on in the world outside of my school.

It is worth noting that in responding to the question about limitations, the principals seldom mentioned inadequate instructional and curricular skills, community relations, or program evaluation. Also, the area of student discipline was not mentioned once by any principal as a possible limitation.

The most common response of the "significant others" in regard to their perceptions of the limitations of the principal was that he had none. There were some minority trends, however. The limitation of the principal most frequently cited by the central office/school board group related to the principal's personality, including being defensive, abrasive, impatient, impetuous, rigid, or lacking confidence. It should be noted, however, that a majority of the principals were not characterized by the central office and school board in this manner. Other limitations mentioned by the central office and school board included not meeting central office expectations and principal conflicts with the school board.

In the case of the other three groups, there was also no majority trend as to limitations of the principal. However, for both students and teachers, the most frequently cited limitation of the principal was his lack of visibility and accessibility, and for the parents it was the principal's lack of follow-through, and too strong a personality. Lack of principal accessibility was also a limitation identified by a number of parents.

In general, the "significant others" cited fewer weaknesses than strengths of the principal. However, in many cases they appeared to be either not knowledgeable about the limitations of the principal or reluctant to mention them. The group that was most knowledgeable, or at least most willing to discuss the limitations of the principal, was the central office/school board group, which tended to be most critical of the principal, followed by the teachers, then the students, and finally the parents.

The Principalship: Satisfactions, Contributions, and   **49**
Needed Improvement

With only a couple of exceptions of hedging or "no comment," the principals seemed satisfied that the principalship today offers good opportunities for leadership. The factors that contributed to their positive attitude about the principalship varied among the principals. However, perhaps the most common theme permeating their comments was that the principalship gives an individual a good opportunity to influence people and to bring about change and improvement in the educational program of the school. As one principal commented,

"This is where the action is and where the young people are." Another principal observed that there is "much opportunity to influence people and situations."

However, in spite of these opportunities, the principals had some definite ideas about how the principalship could be improved. While there was no majority viewpoint, the most frequent response to the question about how the principalship might become a more effective leadership position was to select better people for the position, individuals who possess greater potential or capacity for leadership. The second most common recommendation was to involve the principal more in the development of district policies and decisions, reduce the stifling conditions of too much red tape and bureaucracy, and provide the principal with greater autonomy at the building level so that he could function more as an educational leader.

When asked what, in general, was needed to make the job of principal more manageable and effective, the principals most frequently cited *role clarification* as the number one need. This need took different forms, ranging from a recommendation that the legal status of the principal should be improved, to a feeling that there should be better understanding and recognition of the principal's job by the staff, community, and in particular the central office.

Principals also felt that in order to make the job more manageable and effective, they needed additional administrative and secretarial support and a reduction in the amount of paper work and unnecessary meetings. Although mentioned not so frequently, principals also felt that they needed less interference and more autonomy within the school district, and better background and training in educational leadership. In regard to the latter, the most common recommendation for improving the preservice education of principals was that the preparation program include an internship (interpersonal intercommunications and human relations were also thought to be important), and that, in terms of inservice education for principals, there needed to be more opportunity for principals to discuss common problems and to share ideas.

50

In order to obtain perspective and ideas from a variety of sources on how the job of the principal could be improved and made more effective, the "significant others" were also asked this same question.

Interestingly, and somewhat dishearteningly, the most common response of the "significant others" to the question of how the job of the principal could be improved and made more effective, was that they did not know. Students offered the fewest ideas, followed by parents, then teachers, and finally the central office. Whether this means that the "significant others" believed that the principalship was already effective and could not be improved, or they simply didn't have any ideas for improving the position, is not known.

In those situations in which recommendations for improving the job of principal were offered, the most frequent suggestion by students was that the principal needed to spend more time with students. Teachers, on the other hand, felt that to improve the job of the principal he should get more involved in teaching and show more support and understanding of teachers. The most frequent recommendation from parents for improving the job of the principal was that he should provide greater parent participation. The central office group felt that an improved budget, more autonomy and flexibility, additional administrative assistance, and a better job definition would improve the job of the principal and make it more effective.

The final question asked of the principals in this section was, "When you leave this school, what will you consider your main contributions to have been?" Although the responses of the principals were diverse, the two most common themes pervading the data were: (1) that the principal had brought stability to a very rocky and trouble-filled situation; and (2) that the principal had improved the educational climate and program of the school. Improving in some way the school environment *for students* seemed to be the contribution for which the principals most wanted to be remembered.

The Future

Each principal was asked, "What do you see as conditions, either within schools or in society, that are likely to have significant influence upon you and your school during the next three to five years?" Since it was an open-ended question, the responses were many and varied, but by far the largest single category of perceived influences pertained to public demands upon the schools—demands for more emphasis on the basics, more accountability, more competency or proficiency testing, and higher graduation requirements. Other influences that were mentioned frequently were the general economy, especially as it affects school finance, and enrollment changes. Desegregation and student behavior problems (e.g., nonattendance and drug use) were also stated several times.

When asked what the effects each influence named would have on youth and on schools, the principals frequently made the following comments:

- Emphasis on Basics—There were differences of opinion as to whether this new emphasis is a good thing, but those who had misgivings predicted less innovativeness, more structured programs, less emphasis on subjects and activities other than the "basics," and more teaching to the tests.

- More Accountability—Here again, the principals differed as to whether the pressures for more accountability would produce better education. Those taking the negative view mentioned the

51

likelihood of conflicts between teachers and administrators, dangers in using student achievement tests to measure teachers' effectiveness, less emphasis on affective education and more on that which can be quantified easily, and more court cases challenging the schools to produce results.

- Competency or Proficiency Testing and Higher Graduation Requirements—The principals were again split among those favoring and those opposing this movement. Predictions included the following: There will be more legislation mandating attainment of skills before graduation; schools will have to identify essential competencies; there will be less "social promotion," and underachievers will be identified and remediation will take place before the ninth grade.

- School Finance and General Economy—Here the predictions tended to be on the gloomy side, including reduced budgets, loss of jobs, program cutbacks (especially "frills"), larger classes, and more school closures.

- Enrollment Changes—Although some of the principals predicted larger enrollments in their own schools, the general expectation was for decreases in enrollments, resulting in fewer courses and programs, less diversity in offerings, and reductions in staff, especially among the newer teachers. Some principals spoke pessimistically of the effects of layoffs of younger teachers and nonemployment of new teachers, referring to the innovativeness and involvement in activities that they associate with the behavior of younger teachers.

- Desegregation—Few principals spoke of the positive aspects of desegregation, even though many of the schools in the study were noted for having dealt with desegregation problems in constructive ways. There was rather general agreement that desegregation makes the principal's job more difficult, especially in dealing with conflict and defending against legal action. Some principals spoke of the impact of desegregation on academic standards, and some were concerned about their inability to integrate minority students into the school's social life and activity program.

- Student Behavior Problems—Several principals predicted more stringent school board policies and more rigidity in court decisions dealing with student behavior.

When asked for the source of their information when making their predictions of the future, most of the principals spoke of the professional literature. Discussions with knowledgeable people were also cited by a majority of the principals. Several mentioned popular literature and the mass media, and a few referred to studies and projections made in the local school district or other districts.

The principals were asked what preparations are being made in their schools to meet any of the conditions that they had named. Some of those who had mentioned decreasing enrollments referred to such measures as reductions in staff, moving the ninth grade to the high school, organizing courses into larger blocks in order to concentrate students and maintain programs, busing students, and employing teachers with more than one specialty. Some of the principals who anticipated increasing enrollments spoke of such moves as organizing a quarter system to utilize personnel and facilities during the summer, and planning new buildings.

Responses to "back to the basics," proficiency testing, and accountability pressures included setting up committees or task forces to make studies and recommendations, establishing new programs in such fields as math and English, setting up new aptitude and achievement test programs, and adding new staff.

Some of the principals who cited school finance and general economy problems said that they are conserving wherever they can, devoting more time than ever to development of the budget, and working with school boards, teachers, and other administrators to influence legislation.

About half of the principals stated that they do not use formal surveying as a data-gathering process. Of those who do use such surveys, almost all involve staff members, and several involve parents and students.

The principals were asked whether changes in society that will likely affect schools can be identified by principals, and if so, whether they can prepare their schools for such changes. Most of the principals indicated that they can identify societal trends and can act to prepare their schools for them. Some examples that were given included population growth or decline, the energy shortage, integration, and the decreasing work week. In these and several other cases, one or more principals cited examples of actions that were or could be taken to deal with the changing situation.

Most of the principals expressed the opinion that the media play an important role in changing the school. Examples of both positive and negative influence were given. On the one hand, the media were praised for informing people concerning the schools and arousing their interest in school affairs. On the other hand, the media were criticized by a few of the principals for being non-supportive, inaccurate, and sensational.

What will principals most need in the future in order to succeed? A wide variety of thoughts were expressed. An important category of response included needed skills, which will require better preservice and inservice training as well as experience on the job. Another significant category included the need for stronger support by leaders at local, state, and national levels. Several principals expressed a need for better attitudes on the part of students and parents, and several others said that more help will be needed in the form of personnel and finances.

54

7 The Effective Principal

THIS STUDY WAS DESIGNED as an in-depth look at the effective principal. Its central purpose was to identify personal qualities, professional behavior, and situational factors associated with being an effective high school principal.

Recognizing the complexity of the role, however, and the diversity of research data collected, this study must be viewed as exploratory and its conclusions tentative. Some interesting patterns emerge—call them central tendencies—that provide clues about effectiveness as well as furnish leads for further investigation into specific pieces of the total puzzle. These findings provide interesting observations about the principalship, as well as suggest recommendations for improving the effectiveness of the role. But no final and fully definitive profile of the effective principal is presented.

Perhaps the main factor that characterizes the principals in this study is their diversity. Certain behavioral patterns can be seen in the exemplary principals that are somewhat different from those of principals in general, but the range in almost every trait or behavior category is extensive. This finding would seem to support the situational and contingency models of leadership and cast additional doubt on the notion that there is a single set of personal qualities or a unique leadership style that is effective for all situations.

One major conclusion which can be drawn from the findings of this study, however, is that the majority of principals interviewed are hardworking, dedicated individuals, concerned about students and involved in improving opportunities for learning in their schools.

These principals are also people oriented, their strongest asset being an ability to work with different kinds of people having various needs, interests, and expectations. They seem to understand people, know how to motivate them, and know how to deal effectively with their problems. It is primarily this factor, rather than a technical expertise, that caused the "significant others" to perceive these principals as accessible and effective administrators.

Another major factor which apparently contributes to the principals' effectiveness is an environment of strong support from students, teachers, parents, and the district office along with a reasonable amount of autonomy and resources for performing responsibilities. Although the principals of this study seem to be faced with the same kinds of constraints and limitations as most other principals, these negative factors appear of lower intensity, and the exemplary principals seem better able to cope with them. Therefore, it appears that to increase the effectiveness of the principalship, adequate autonomy, resources, and support are important prerequisites.

Several findings of the study warrant special attention. Many of the principals complain about the excessive amount of paperwork demanded of them, their required attendance at numerous district meetings, and the lack of clarity in their job descriptions. While much of the paperwork and many of the meetings may be absolutely necessary, it would seem that these areas and the principal's role expectations need re-examination by the district office in cooperation with the building administrators.

A related area of concern is the data which show that most of the effective principals are not planning to stay in the principalship. This may suggest that the job isn't as satisfying as it might be. Or it could reflect a natural ambition that is typically associated with individuals who would like higher status or a more challenging job. In any regard, the continuing attrition of effective individuals from the principalship does not bode well for the position today or tomorrow.

In addition, it should be recognized that although the "significant others" are very positive about the effectiveness of these principals, the findings of the study also indicate that the "significant others" are not knowledgeable about many aspects of the principal's job and job performance. Their ratings of the principal are based primarily on *impressions* of the extent to which the principal is meeting their expectations rather than on concrete information.

Since the data from the study also show principals to have a less than complete awareness of the issues and problems as viewed by students, parents, and teachers, it can be hypothesized that the positive ratings of the principals' effectiveness by the "significant others" may be grounded on a shifting confidence base which could erode under adverse conditions.

The principalship, to some extent, is like the classic Japanese film "Rashomon," where an incident involving four participants resulted in four different versions in testimony to the judge. Each version tended to project the personal interests of the individuals involved. So it is that teachers, students, parents, and the central office, as well as the principal—each has somewhat differing views of the principalship as it is lived day by day. All referent groups are supportive—of these effective principals at least—but views differ about what makes the principalship go well, about what the principal does in a typical work week, about how he goes about tasks, and about the relative contribution of each group to the total success of the school.

Moving beyond these summary observations, a more detailed analysis of some specific factors associated with effective principals provides additional insight. Each area is discussed in some detail beginning with personal factors.

Personal Factors

While findings from the present study tend to support an abundance of previous research indicating that effective leaders cannot be identified merely by assessing personal histories, the current and past records of the 60 exemplary principals *as a group* do reveal certain patterns. Thirty percent of the exemplary principals have doctorates, with another 17 percent earning degrees at the education specialist level. This indicates these principals to be a well-educated group. As undergraduates, they tended to be very active in extracurricular activities, especially athletics, with 60 percent of the group participating—although few were coaches later. Only a few of the 60 achieved high academic recognition; five were graduated cum laude and two were Phi Beta Kappa.

Apparently job mobility is a characteristic of the exemplary principals. Only one-third of the group stepped from teacher to administrator in the same district.

Very active in community affairs, especially in churches and service clubs and in various professional organizations at the local, state, and national levels, the principals regard this involvement as quite useful.

The Principal and the Job

In general, the exemplary principal's work habits are demanding, although great variations exist among individuals. The average work day is approximately 9½ hours, in addition to three nights per week on school business. Many of these principals also devote part of their weekends to the job.

Although their daily activities appear to be influenced by things that "just come up," the principals generally follow their intended plans in each of the nine task areas. They were vague, however, in describing the planning processes actually followed. Their testimony suggests a highly idiosyncratic process. Principals do spend more time on student behavior and school management than they would prefer to spend in those task areas.

The "significant others," with some exceptions, are in fairly close agreement with the principals as to the way time is spent. However, the

57

agreement concerning time actually spent may be more apparent than real, since many of the "significant others" lack knowledge about the principal's use of time or hours of work.

Each group of "significant others" tends to view the school and the principal from a slightly different perspective, even though much agreement exists among the groups and with the principal. For example, teachers are inclined to feel that principals spend too much time on district office matters, but this feeling is not shared by superintendents and board members. Generally speaking, however, the exemplary principals operate in a highly supportive situation with all referent groups.

The Principal and Students

Informal communication is the key to the principal's relationship with students. Being visible, visiting with students in a positive, enthusiastic manner in the halls and cafeteria, at school activities, and in other informal settings, is common with effective principals. Meetings with student leaders typically pertained to extracurricular activities and student behavior, but not often to instructional and curriculum matters.

Student leaders and the principals tended to perceive the main school-connected concerns of students somewhat differently. The principals were more inclined to cite student concerns about school activities, school spirit, autonomy, peer relations, the quality of instruction, and preparation for college and jobs. Teachers also generally held this view. The student leader's perceptions of student concerns, joined by parents and the central office groups, concentrated upon the areas of college and jobs. This would seem to reflect a seriousness of purpose beyond the school campus not entirely appreciated by the professional staff.

The principals regard the involvement of students in decisions to be crucial, although much of the involvement is on an informal basis. Being available, listening, being interested in students' views, and taking them into account when making decisions—these are characteristic patterns of behavior of many of the principals.

The predominant image that the principals want to project to students is one of being "firm but fair."

The Principal and the Community/Parents

Although the parents or other community groups are not regularly involved in curriculum planning in most of the schools, the principals believe they know the community's concerns. Several utilize advisory groups on an ad hoc basis. As with the students' views, the parents' and other citizens' views are most often received by the principals on an informal basis rather than through formal surveys or meetings.

The Principal and the Staff

The exemplary principals regard their own actions to be important to good school climate and teacher morale. This is manifested especially by giving strong support to teachers, by involving teachers in important decisions, and by open communication. Most of the interviewed teachers agreed with this observation.

The principals appear to meet more frequently with staff groups than with student or parent groups. These staff meetings are primarily with the faculty as a whole and with department chairpersons, or with cabinet and administrative staff members. An "open door" policy was cited often by teachers as well as principals.

Most of the principals look favorably upon master contracts, although several disadvantages as well as advantages were cited. The majority are not involved in negotiating contracts with teachers. Only 12 of the 60 principals reported that grievances had been filed within the past year.

The Principal and the Curriculum/Programs

In the development of curriculum and programs, except for the implementation of decisions that are mandated from higher up in the school district, the process usually begins in the departments, where plans are originated and developed and where evaluation is done. The faculty as a whole prioritizes goals, discusses plans, and reviews progress. The central office provides district-wide goals and plans, consultant assistance, resources, and final approval. With few exceptions, students, parents, and community groups are not significantly involved in the process.

The "significant others" were not knowledgeable about the processes used by the principal to plan major projects or programs.

The diversity of course offerings was frequently mentioned by principals and by "significant others" as the major strength of the school's program.

The Principal as Problem Solver

The principals and the "significant others" were in agreement that the principals are effective problem solvers. The principals were especially confident in the areas of student discipline and extracurricular programs, but less confident about evaluating teacher performance. The "significant others" groups had difficulty in identifying specific problems that the principals did *not* handle well.

Three different approaches to problem solving were described: (1) utilizing the principles and steps recommended in the professional literature; (2) emphasizing personal qualities such as listening, staying "cool," being able to take pressure, and being persistent; and (3) utilizing an intuitive approach. Most of the principals do not employ the

59

"scientific process" of problem solving found in the professional literature. Instead, they rely on their intuition and personal qualities to solve problems.

The "significant others" are not particularly knowledgeable about the problem-solving process employed by the principal. They are primarily interested in the *results* achieved, tending to judge the principal's effectiveness in terms of outcomes rather than processes, especially as those outcomes meet their particular expectations.

Personal and Professional Outlook

Almost all principals expressed the feeling that the job offers a good opportunity for leadership and significant service. However, they tend to be upwardly mobile, with one-half not planning to stay indefinitely in their present positions. The most common career goal is the superintendency, with college teaching the second most popular aspiration.

According to the principals, incompetent and undedicated teachers are the greatest irritation. The "significant others" agree, and also perceive the principals to be bothered by student misbehavior and parent apathy.

Role clarification was cited by the principals as the main avenue through which the job could be made more manageable and effective. They also mentioned additional administrative and secretarial assistance, less paper work, and fewer meetings to attend.

For most of the principals, stress is not seen as a major problem. When stress does occur, the most frequently mentioned method of dealing with it is to get away from the office and walk around or engage in some form of recreation. Surprisingly few of the principals cope with stress by talking over their problems with others.

The principals as well as the "significant others" regard personal qualities rather than professional expertise to be the principal's main strengths. They consider the ability to relate well to people to be their greatest asset. The "significant others" see the principals as strong in oral communication and effective in one-to-one situations.

60

The most frequently stated recommendations by the principals for making the principalship more effective were: (1) select better people for the position; (2) get principals more involved in the development of district policies and procedures; and (3) give principals greater autonomy to function as educational leaders. The exemplary principals overwhelmingly support the internship as the one most effective way to improve the preservice training of principals.

The Principal as a Change Agent

The principals tend to see themselves as initiators or facilitators of change, but seldom as consultants or evaluators. The "significant others" perceive the principals as initiating change less frequently than the principals report involvement in change. The principal's contribution may be invisible to the majority of clientele. Each referent group tends to rate itself higher for contributing to change than it is rated by the other groups.

A composite of the change strategy used by the 60 principals would include the following: (1) recognize the need and plant the seed with staff members and/or others; (2) work with people, especially those most affected—but do not impose change; (3) provide needed resources and support.

The Principal and the Future

The exemplary principals foresee demands for more emphasis on the basics, more accountability, more proficiency or competency testing, and tougher graduation requirements. Changes in the general economy and enrollment decline were also mentioned frequently.

The principals believe that changes in society likely to affect schools can be identified and that schools can prepare for such changes. They gave many examples of having met similar challenges in the past.

The Principal's Effectiveness as Seen by Others

Although a halo effect possibly resulted from the 60 principals' being identified as "effective," they did get high ratings from the "significant others" in all categories of performance. The community parent groups tend to rate the principals highest on curriculum matters, accessibility, change, and parent-community relations. The students give the highest ratings on change, staff relations, and evaluation. The faculty members' highest ratings pertain to parent-community relations, accessibility, evaluation, and change. The superintendent/school board leaders mark the principals uniformly high on almost all categories—only slightly lower on change than on the other areas.

Recommendations

1. The exemplary principals generally view excessive paperwork and required attendance at district level meetings to be major problems with regard to their time. Teachers agree with this view.

   These are problems which seem to be pervasive in the principalship and demand local, state, and national attention. Although most of the principals see many opportunities for significant leadership and service in the position, the fact that many of them do not plan to stay in the principalship very long suggests that the job isn't as attractive as it might be. Local school boards, superintendents, professional administrator organizations, universities, and all other interested groups need to work individually and cooperatively to ameliorate these problems and others before they have an even more serious effect on the principalship.

2. Because the principals perceive a major need for role clarification, it behooves school boards, superintendents, professional organizations, universities, parent groups, and others related to the principalship to work hard at making the position more clearly and broadly understood. If ambiguity about expectations are frustrating to effective principals, they must be even more troublesome to principals in general.

3. Since even the effective principals can misjudge the issues that are of concern to "significant others," who in turn reveal a lack of knowledge about most aspects of the principal's performance, it would appear that there is a need to improve communication between the principals and the other groups.

   Although the principals seem to accomplish much through informal communication, it would be advisable for them to develop and utilize some more formal mechanisms for achieving two-way communication to supplement the informal methods now employed. Since apparently the referent groups know little about program initiatives taken by principals, perhaps planning committees formed annually to improve the school program would serve the purpose of informing these groups about the principal's interest in instruction as well as providing an opportunity for joint communication. Also, it can be projected that since advisory groups may operate on a very thin knowledge base, part of any advisory group's responsibility must be to know more about the position it is to advise.

4. The data from the study strongly support the conclusion that training in program evaluation, curriculum development, school/community communications, teacher inservice education, and time management needs greater attention in the pre-and inservice programs of administrators. Unless administrators improve their skills in these areas, the strong support of "significant others" may evaporate.

5. Departments of school administration should make the recruitment and selection of promising candidates a top priority. The exemplary principals cited the selection of more able people for the principalship as the best way to make the job more effective, and much other evidence supports this view. This conclusion is further supported by the finding in this study that effectiveness in human relations—a skill that is difficult to acquire through training—was seen as the outstanding characteristic of the exemplary principals. It is further supported by the finding in this study that limitations in personality characteristics—which are also difficult to eliminate through train-

ing—were viewed as the category of weakness most often perceived in the principals.

Although effective recruitment and selection are probably the best means of ensuring that principals will possess appropriate personality characteristics and human relations skills, more attention also needs to be given in the university preparation program to the development of these skills and characteristics.

6. Most of the principals and many others regard the internship to be a highly important component of preservice preparation programs, along with simulation and other "real life" learning activities. Learning theory also supports such learning activities. More emphasis should be placed on these components. Universities and principals' organizations should seek better ways to combine their resources in order to make preservice training more effective. The University Council for Educational Administration (UCEA) should be involved in these efforts.

7. Problems pertaining to teacher performance are the ones most often cited by the principals as being ineffectively handled. More thought should be given to this task area in the planning of preservice and inservice education for principals.

8. Finally, the findings of this study raise certain questions that suggest a need for further investigation. For example, we need to know more about the problem-solving processes of effective high school principals; about the relevancy of certain career ladders to the performance of effective principals; and about differing perceptions of a principals' behavior as it varies from teacher to student to parent to central office. Further light is needed on these and other variables which contribute to the effectiveness of the building administrator.

Appendix A

_____
Date

INTERVIEW GUIDE

PRINCIPALS

DATA SHEET 1: PRINCIPAL-SCHOOL INFORMATION

_____   _____
      Name of Principal   High School

_____ _____ _____   _____
  Age   Sex   Race   Street Address, High School

(___)   (___)   _____
Telephone, Office Telephone, Home   City   State   Zip

_____   _____
    Name of Superintendent   Street Address, Central Office

_____ _____   _____
District Enrollment Number of   City   State   Zip
(Approx., as of now) High Schools
                     in District

DATA FOR YOUR SCHOOL

Current Enrollment _____

No. of Teachers, Full Time: _____   No. of Teachers, Part Time: _____

No. of Counselors, Full Time: ____   No. of Counselors, Part Time: ____

Number of Administrative Staff, full time equivalency _____
(Asst principals, deans, activity directors, etc.)

How adequate is the amount of help provided you by the administrative
staff? (if any)

        Completely adequate ____   Usually adequate   ____
        Somewhat inadequate ____   Completely inadequate ____

        Comments:

Number of department or area chairmen with at least one period of
   released time per day for chairmanship: _____

How adequate is the amount of help provided you via department or area chairmen? (if any)

Completely adequate _____   Usually adequate _____

Somewhat inadequate _____   Completely inadequate _____

Comments:

Student body: _____% _____% _____% _____% _____% _____% _____%
                White   Black Chicano Asian American Other   Other
                                  or   Indian (Identify)
                               Hispanic

Types of Programs by approximate percentage of student body
  (Must add to 100%)
                                          <u>Comments</u>

College Prep   _____
Vocational/Business   _____
General   _____
Other (specify)   _____

What percentages of your junior and senior classes are in these kinds
  of <u>community experience</u> programs:

Work study   _____%   Alternative programs _____%
Released time   _____%   Other (specify)   _____%
Community service   _____%

65

_____ Number

DATA SHEET 2: PRINCIPAL-PERSONAL INFORMATION

Education

Degree	Institution	Date Completed (yr)	Major Field
_____	_____	_____	_____
_____	_____	_____	_____
_____	_____	_____	_____
_____	_____	_____	_____

Other voluntary formal training totaling at least 3 days per program: (since January 1973)	Duration (weeks)	Offered by: (NASSP, state, college, etc.)
_____	_____	_____
_____	_____	_____
_____	_____	_____
_____	_____	_____
_____	_____	_____

Activities or Athletics in college: _____

_____

Honors or Awards in College: _____

_____

Non Educational Honors, Awards, Activities: _____

_____

_____

_____

66

Teaching Experience

School	Place	Subject/Level	School Year
_____	_____	_____	_____
_____	_____	_____	_____
_____	_____	_____	_____
_____	_____	_____	_____

School Administrative Experience

School	Place	Title	School Year
_____	_____	_____	_____
_____	_____	_____	_____
_____	_____	_____	_____
_____	_____	_____	_____

Work Experience (since Bachelor's Degree), full time only, including military:

Type of Work	Employer	Months
_____	_____	_____
_____	_____	_____
_____	_____	_____
_____	_____	_____
_____	_____	_____

67

Professional Memberships

Organization	How Active Are You?			How Useful Is Membership?			Why?
	Very	Mod.	Not	Very	Mod.	Not	
NASSP	___	___	___	___	___	___	_____
State Pr. Assn.	___	___	___	___	___	___	_____
AASA	___	___	___	___	___	___	_____
ASCD	___	___	___	___	___	___	_____
Phi Delta Kappa	___	___	___	___	___	___	_____
_____	___	___	___	___	___	___	_____

Professional Activity

What professional activities have you been involved with since January 1973 (speaking, teaching, writing, etc.)?

_____

_____

_____

Memberships in Community Organizations (Church, Civic, etc.)

Organization	How Active Are You?			How Useful Is Membership?			Why?
	Very	Mod.	Not	Very	Mod.	Not	
_____	___	___	___	___	___	___	_____
_____	___	___	___	___	___	___	_____
_____	___	___	___	___	___	___	_____
_____	___	___	___	___	___	___	_____

Current family status: Married ___, Single ___, Divorced ___, Widowed ___

DATA SHEET 3: JOB

1. What is the length of your work year: 10 months ___ , 11 months ___ .

2. What type of contract do you have:

    1 year ___   2 year ___   Continuous ___

    Other (explain) _____

3. What are your typical school hours; i.e., on a typical school day, when do you arrive at your office and when do you leave the office for home?

    Arrive at school _____   Leave school for home _____

4. Over the past two weeks, did you schedule time on your calendar for certain tasks? Listed below are nine functional areas. Indicate the number of hours (if any) that you prescheduled yourself into each of the nine functional areas listed below:

Area of Activity	Hours Prescheduled (planned)	Hours Actually Spent
Program development (curriculum, instructional leadership)	_____	_____
Personnel (evaluation, advising, conferencing, recruiting)	_____	_____
School management (weekly calendar, office, budget, correspondence, memos, etc.)	_____	_____
Student activities (meetings, supervision, planning)	_____	_____
Student behavior (discipline, attendance, meetings	_____	_____
Community (PTA, advisory groups, parent conferences)	_____	_____
District office (meetings, task forces, reports, etc.)	_____	_____
Professional development (reading, conferences, etc.	_____	_____
Planning (annual, long range)	_____	_____

If scheduled time is taken for other things, what typically causes the interruptions?

_____

_____

_____

69

With whom do you typically work in long range planning for your school? Check all that provide significant assistance:

___ assistant administrators, ___ central office, ___ counselors,

___ teacher committees, ___ department or division chairpersons,

___ students, ___ consultants, ___ fellow principals, ___ parents,

___ community committees, ___ county or state agencies, ___ others

(describe)_____

5. How do you spend your time during the work year? Rank the nine functional areas according to the amounts of time spent in each area. (No. 1 signifies greatest amount of time, No. 9 signifies least amount of time.)

    Also, rank the areas according to how you feel that you should spend your professional time (would like to spend the time).

DO Spend Time	Area of Activity	SHOULD Spend Time
____	Program Development	____
____	Personnel	____
____	School Management	____
____	Student Activities	____
____	Student Behavior	____
____	Community	____
____	District Office	____
____	Professional Development	____
____	Planning	____

6. What factors determine this distribution of time?

    _____

    _____

    _____

7. In a typical week, how many nights are you away from home for at least an hour on school-connected business?

    _____ Nights   How many last week? _____

    What typically is the nature of these meetings or events?

8. Do you work on weekends? If so, what are the most typical tasks?

    _____

9. What factors or people determine what it is you are going to do on
    a typical day? Rank order the influence of each factor.

    ____ I plan in advance. ____ Weekly cycle of responsibilities.

    ____ Things just come up. ____ Supervisor assigns tasks.

    ____ Inbasket. ____ Other _____.

10. When and how do you plan for what you are going to do the following
    week?

    Time of planning _____. Process of planning _____.

11. Identify in order of importance three factors or constraints that
    make your job more difficult than it should be.

12. Identify in order of importance three facets or aspects of the job
    situation which enable you to be effective as a principal.

13. Do you think any of your time is wasted as a principal? If so, where?

14. What suggestions would you give other principals for coping with
    the problems of not enough time?

15. Do the principals negotiate with the central office on working
    conditions and salary? What role do you play?

71

DATA SHEET 4: TASKS

A. Students

1. How frequently do you meet with student leaders?
    _____ Daily   _____ Weekly   _____ Monthly
    _____ Twice weekly   _____ Biweekly

2. With what student leaders do you meet frequently?

    _____ Cabinet members   _____ Informal leaders

    _____ Class officers or   _____ Club leaders
          Student Council officers

    _____ Special Advisory Groups   _____ Others (specify)

3. What was the typical content of such meetings in recent months?

    _____ Activities, projects   _____ Student discipline

    _____ School rules   _____ Student-community problems

    _____ Curriculum   _____ Teaching quality

    _____ Student-teacher relations _____ Student-student relations

    _____ Others (specify)_____

4. When you wish to influence student behavior in positive directions
    what initiatives do you take? (if any)

5. What role do you play in implementing these initiatives?

6. What would you say are the main school-connected concerns of

    your students? _____

7. What would you say are the main non-school concerns of your

    students? _____

8. How do you keep informed about what your students are thinking

    concerning school or about life in general? _____

    _____

9. What do you see as your primary role with regard to students?

72

10. How would you like (hope) to be perceived by students in your role as principal? _____

_____

11. What do you think should be your school's major contributions to the lives of your students? _____

_____

B. Community/Parents

1. With what parent groups do you meet regularly or frequently?

	Group	Frequency
_____	PTA/Parent Organization	_____
_____	PTA Executive Committee	_____
_____	Parent task forces	_____
_____	Parent Advisory Groups	_____
_____	Boosters Club	_____
_____	Voc/Spec. Ed. Advisory	_____
_____	Other (specify)_____	_____
_____	Other (specify)_____	_____

2. Over the past several months, what have been the main concerns of parents' groups with whom you have met? _____

_____

3. Over the past several months, with what community groups or agencies have you had significant contact? _____

_____

4. What was the nature of these contacts (#3 above)? _____

_____

5. Do community persons or organizations participate in curriculum planning for your school? Yes ___; No ___. If so, describe the process.

6. In what other ways do community organizations or agencies influence your school? With what community groups do you typically meet?

73

7. In what areas do you try to involve parents or other citizens in the school?

____Set objectives, priorities   ____Aides

____Evaluation   ____Curriculum advisory

____Finance   ____Personnel criteria/selection

____Student Rights/Resp.   ____Other

____Resource persons

8. Have you taken initiatives over the past three years to increase parent/citizen participation? Explain.

9. What methods do you employ for communicating with parents and the general community?

10. What methods do you employ to seek feedback from parents and the rest of the community?

C. Staff

1. With what staff groups do you meet regularly or frequently?

Group	Frequency
____Faculty as a whole	_____
____Department chairpersons	_____
____Cabinet/Senate	_____
____Curriculum council	_____
____Secretaries, clerks	_____
____Special task forces	_____
____Other (specify)_____	_____
____Other (specify)_____	_____

2. What are the main issues/concerns of the teachers in this high school?

____ salaries   ____ staff evaluation

____ student behavior   ____ insufficient clerical help

____ class size   ____ inadequate instructional materials

____ insufficient time   ____ ineffective administration

____ lack of public support   ____ student grading & reporting

        ____ others (specify) _____

3. What causes good school morale/good school climate? What part do you play in this?

4. What specific initiatives, if any, have you taken the last three
    years to provide or improve faculty inservice education?

5. What do you see as the advantages and disadvantages of adminis-
    tering a school with a master contract (negotiated agreement)?

6. How would you characterize the faculty's influence in the
    decision-making process in this high school?

1	.	2	.	3	.	4	.	5
not at all influential				somewhat influential				highly influential

7. How much involved are you in the process of negotiations
    (consultation, bargaining) with teachers?

1	.	2	.	3	.	4	.	5
no involvement				some involvement				high involvement

8. How do you think your teachers perceive you with regard to their
    position in negotiations?

1	.	2	.	3	.	4	.	5
not supportive				somewhat supportive				highly supportive

9. How effective do you regard yourself to be in the area of
    staff relations?

1	.	2	.	3	.	4	.	5
highly ineffective				highly effective				highly effective

10. If a grievance has been filed in your school in the past year,
    please describe the issue and the process:

    _____

    _____

    _____

    _____

D. Curriculum/Programs

    1. We are interested in the ways that curriculum is developed in
        your school (participants and processes). Please give us an
        example of a new program developed recently.

Participant	Role	Process (summarize)
____ Central Office	_____	
____ High School Staff	_____	
____ Departments	_____	
____ Curriculum Committees	_____	
____ Students	_____	

_____ Parents   _____

_____ Community Groups   _____

_____ Consultants   _____

_____ Others (specify)   _____

2. What process do you use in planning major projects and programs?

    _____ Recognizing the occasion   _____ Providing for resources

    _____ Establishing needs   _____ Providing for evaluation

    _____ Defining goals/objectives   _____ Providing for training

    _____ Organizing   _____ Securing allegiances

              _____ Other (specify) _____

3. What is your role in curriculum development?

4. What professional resources do you normally rely upon for
    curriculum/program improvement? (consultants, periodicals, etc.)

5. By whom are curricular changes normally initiated?

    _____ individual teachers   _____ central administration
    _____ departments   _____ building administration
    _____ students & parents   _____ Others (specify) _____

6. What do you consider to be the major strengths of this high
    school with regard to its curriculum/programs?

7. What do you consider to be the major weaknesses of this high
    school with regard to its curriculum/programs?

8. How do you anticipate curriculum needs from year to year?
    How do you organize resources to meet those needs?

9. How effective do you regard yourself to be in the area of
    curriculum development?

        1   .   2   .   3   .   4   .   5
    ineffective   somewhat   highly
                         effective   effective

    Explain.

10. What is your role, if any, in the development of extracurricular
    activities?

E. Program Evaluation

1. How do you evaluate the outcomes of programs or projects initiated by you?

2. Other than the evaluation that is required by others (such as the central administration, the state department of education, or accreditation groups), are special efforts made to evaluate all programs in this high school on a regular basis?

3. Who is significantly involved in evaluating programs in this school?

    ____ central office personnel   ____ students

    ____ high school administrators   ____ parents

    ____ teachers   ____ others (specify)

                                       _____

4. How do you usually provide for the evaluation of major events/ projects/programs?

    ____ Seeing that evaluation is part of plans

    ____ Administering reactionaire to participants at end of process

    ____ Using external evaluators

    ____ Gathering product measures

    ____ Monitoring processes systematically

    ____ Others (specify) _____

5. How effective do you regard yourself to be in the area of program evaluation?

        1   .   2   .   3   .   4   .   5
     _____
       highly   somewhat   highly
     ineffective   effective   effective

6. What outside resources do you use to assist with planning?

    _____

    _____

    _____

    _____

77

DATA SHEET 5: PROBLEM-SOLVING AND PROBLEM ATTACK

All high school principals, sooner or later, have to deal with difficult problems.

1. Can you name a problem that you feel you handled well?

    How did it arise? (What events occurred?)

    What did you do?

    How did the problem get resolved?

    (Ask for description of second problem—one should be "internal" with students or staff, one should be "external" with community, district office or media.)

2. Can you name a problem that you feel you did not handle well?

    How did it arise? (What events occurred?)

    What did you do?

    How did the problem get resolved?

3. How effective do you regard yourself in the area of problem solving?

1	.	2	.	3	.	4	.	5
highly ineffective				somewhat effective				highly effective

4. What do you consider the most important components of problem resolution?

    _____

    _____

5. How do you determine when to make a decision?

    _____

    _____

78

DATA SHEET 6: CHANGE

1. What major changes occurred in this high school during the past
    year or two in which you played a major role?

    _____ curriculum   _____ student activities

    _____ management   _____ student behavior

    _____ community relations   _____ school climate

    _____ staff relations   _____ other (specify) _____

2. Where did the idea for (one of the above) originate?

    _____ staff   _____ central administration

    _____ students   _____ advisory group

    _____ patrons   _____ principal

           _____ others (specify) _____

3. Was there a source of resistance? _____

4. What is your typical role in the changes that occur in the high
    school?

    _____ initiator   _____ facilitator

    _____ planner   _____ evaluator

    _____ consultant   _____ others (specify) _____

5. Do you have a particular strategy or approach that you typically
    use to bring about change?
    Yes ____; No ____. If so, please describe it.

6. What do you think constitutes good leadership? Give an example.

7. As you know, there have been several national reports in the past
    two or three years on the reform of secondary education in the
    United States. What reports are you acquainted with?

___ The Reform of Secondary Education, Report of National Commission
___ Vitalizing the High School, Assn for Supervision and Curric. Devel.
___ Youth: Transition to Adulthood, President's Panel on Youth
___ New Roles for Youth in the School and Community, Report of National
        Commission on Resources for Youth

79

____ The Education of Adolescents, Report of National Panel on High Schools
     and Adolescent Education
____ RISE, Report of Calif. Commission for Reform of Intermediate and
     Secondary Education
____ The Adolescent, Other Citizens, and Their High Schools, Task Force '74
____ Secondary Schools in a Changing Society: This We Believe, NASSP Task
     Force
____ The Boundless Resource: A Prospectus for an Education/Work Policy,
     National Manpower Institute

     Which ones of these have been particularly useful to you? (identify)

8. Have you used any of these with staff? (explain)

    ____ Circulated   ____ Inservice program

    ____ Faculty meeting   ____ Curriculum reform

    ____ others (explain)   ____ Graduation requirements committee

9. Have these reports had any impact upon the school program? (explain)

10. Identify a change that has been imposed upon you or your school.
    Explain the source of the requirements and your actions in
    response to the requirement.

80

DATA SHEET 7: PERSONAL/PROFESSIONAL

1. Why do you think you were selected for this job?

2. How long do you intend to remain in this high school?
    _____ As long as the district will permit
    _____ Not more than a year or two
    _____ Three to five years
    _____ Six to ten years
    _____ Other (specify) _____

3. What are your long-range career plans?

4. What do you consider to be your major strengths or assets in
    handling this job?

5. What do you consider to be your limitations in handling this job?

6. What things tend to bother you or "get to" you as principal?

7. How do you deal with stress?

8. What are the main institutional (school) and social (society
    constraints) on your job and on secondary education?

9. With whom do you find it helpful and rewarding to share your
    professional problems?

10. Speculate about the high school principalship in general. What
    is needed to make the job more manageable and effective?

11. What suggestions do you have for improving the preservice training of principals?

12. What suggestions do you have for improving the inservice training of principals?

13. Are you satisfied that the principalship today offers you a good opportunity for leadership? (explain)

    How might the principalship become a more effective leadership position?

14. When you leave this school, what will you consider your main contributions have been?

DATA SHEET 8: FUTURE

1. What do you see as conditions, either within schools or in society, that are likely to have significant influence upon you and your school during the next three to five years?

____ Enrollment changes   ____ Finance & general economy

____ Students' nonattendance   ____ Drug use

____ Alternative schools, program   ____ Accountability

____ Demands for basics   ____ New technology

____ Declining achievement   ____ Community participation

____ Compulsory education   ____ Staff competency

____ Community-based learning   ____ Competency testing

____ National youth service   ____ Graduation requirements

____ Desegregation   ____ Other _____

2. What is likely to be the effect on youth and on schools?
    (each one named)

3. Where do you get most of the information that influences your predictions about the future of high schools such as this one?

____ Present events   ____ Professional literature

____ School district projections/   ____ Popular literature
      studies
                          ____ Others (specify)
____ Discussions with knowledge-
      able people   _____

4. What preparations are being made in this high school to meet any of the conditions named?

5. Do you do any formal surveying of staff ___ , parents ___ , students ___ , outside professionals ___ ?
    Others _____ ?   Describe the process.

83

6. Can a principal identify changes or directions in society that will likely affect schools? If so, give an example. Can you prepare your school for these changes? How?

7. What role does the media play (if any) in changing your school?

8. In the future, what will the principal most need in order to succeed?

___ Inservice on new problems   ___ Better student attitudes

___ Experience   ___ Good state & national leadership

___ School reorganization   ___ Strong local leadership

___ Additional administrative help   ___ Stronger professional organization

___ Responsible parents   ___ Other (explain)

_____

Appendix B

_____ Number

Date
_____

INTERVIEW GUIDE

SIGNIFICANT OTHERS

DATA SHEET: JOB

1. What do you think are the principal's typical daily hours on the
    job; i.e., from the time he arrives at school in the morning until
    he leaves to go home? _____ hours.

2. How do you think the principal spent his time during the past week?
    Rank the nine task areas identified below according to the amount
    of time spent in each area, and then according to the way that you
    feel he should spend his time. (No. 1 signifies highest priority
    for time.)

Area of Activity	Time Actually Spent	Your Priorities for Time Spent
Program development (curriculum, instructional leadership)	_____	_____
Personnel (evaluation, advising, conferencing, recruiting)	_____	_____
School management (weekly calendar, office, budget, correspondence, memos, etc.)	_____	_____
Student activities (meetings, supervision, planning)	_____	_____
Student behavior (discipline, attendance, meetings	_____	_____
Community (PTA, advisory groups, parent conferences)	_____	_____
District office (meetings, task forces, reports, etc.)	_____	_____
Professional development (reading, conferences, etc.)	_____	_____
Planning (annual, long range)	_____	_____

3. Some principals are highly accessible ("open door"), whereas others
    are difficult to reach. How would you describe this principal?

    ```
     1    .    2    .    3    .    4    .    5
    extremely                          extremely
    inaccessible                       accessible
    ```

4. What are the school-connected activities that occupy a great deal of
    this principal's time, other than the regular school hours time he
    spends?

5. What conditions of the job are especially helpful to this principal?
    (plenty of assistance ___, supportive central office ___, supportive
    staff ___, supportive community ___, supportive students ___,
    affluent district ___, others (specify) _____)

6. What conditions of the job make it difficult for this principal to
    do as well as he might do otherwise? (not enough help ___, non-
    supportive central office ___, non-supportive staff ___, non-
    supportive community ___, non-supportive students ___, impoverished
    school district ___, others (specify) _____.)

7. What are the most effective means of communication this principal
    uses with teachers and parents?

85

DATA SHEET: TASKS

A. Students

1. As far as you know, does the P meet regularly with student leaders? yes ___ no ___ . If so, how often does he meet with them? daily ___ , weekly ___ , monthly ___ , other (specify)_____ .

2. With what student leaders does he meet? class officers ___ , student council officers ___ , club leaders ___ , others (specify) _____ .

3. What is the typical content of such meetings? (check one or more) curriculum___ , extracurricular activities___ , student government ___ , quality of teaching___ , student behavior___ , others (specify) _____ .

4. What, in your opinion, are the major concerns of the students in this high school?

5. How do principals determine these concerns?

6. How would you describe this P with respect to the way in which he deals with students? (circle one number)

1	.	2	.	3	.	4	.	5
extremely autocratic								extremely democratic

7. What role does the principal play in student activities?

8. What role does the principal take in student discipline?

B. Community/Parents

1. As far as you know, does the P meet regularly with certain groups of parents? yes___ , no___ . If so, what groups? PTA___ , PTA Exec. Committee___ , Parent task forces___ , Parent advisory groups___ , Boosters Club___ , Voc/Spec. Ed. Advisory___ , Others (specify) _____ .

2. When the P meets with parent groups, what do they deal with?

3. Does the P consult with community groups/leaders in curricular planning? often___ , sometimes___ , rarely___ , never___ .

4. How beneficial to the school are the P's meetings with parents and community groups? very helpful___ , somewhat helpful___ , not helpful___ .

5. With respect to this P's effectiveness in working with parents and other community groups, how would you rate him in comparison with other P's you have known?

```
     1      .    2    .    3    .    4    .    5
 _____
 extremely                              extremely
 ineffective                            effective
```

C. Staff

1. As far as you know, with what staff groups does the P meet regularly? faculty as a whole___, department chairpersons___, cabinet/senate___, curriculum council___, secretaries/clerks___, special task forces___, other (specify) _____.

2. How would you characterize the faculty's influence in the decision-making process in this high school?

```
     1      .    2    .    3    .    4    .    5
 _____
 not at all                             highly
 influential                            influential
```

3. What are the main issues/concerns of the teachers in this high school? salaries___, student behavior___, large class size___, insufficient time___, lack of public support___, staff evaluation___, insufficient clerical help___, inadequate instructional materials___, ineffective administration___, student grades___, others (specify) _____.

4. How would you characterize this P's relations with the staff, in comparison with other P's you have known?

```
     1      .    2    .    3    .    4    .    5
 _____
 extremely                              extremely
 ineffective                            effective
```

D. Curriculum/Programs

1. Generally speaking, what groups participate in the process of curriculum development in this high school? central office___, high school staff as a whole___, departments___, curriculum committees___, students___, parents___, community groups___, others (specify) _____.

87

2. What is the principal's role in curriculum development?

3. By whom are curricular changes normally initiated? individual teachers___, departments___, students & parents___, central administration___, building administration___, others (specify) _____.

4. What do you consider to be the major strengths of this high school with regard to its curriculum/programs?

5. What do you consider to be the major weaknesses of this high school with regard to its curriculum/programs?

6. How would you compare this P with others you have known with respect to his role in the development of curriculum?

1	.	2	.	3	.	4	.	5
extremely ineffective								extremely effective

E. Program Planning and Evaluation

1. As far as you know, what process does this P use in planning major events/projects/programs? recognizing the occasion___, establishing needs___, defining goals/objectives___, organizing___, providing for resources___, providing for evaluation___, providing for needed training___, securing allegiances___, others (specify) _____.

2. What outside help does he usually use in planning major events/projects/programs? central administration___, state association___, national association___, university___, other (specify)_____.

3. How does the principal usually provide for the evaluation of major events/projects/programs? seeing that evaluation is part of the plans___, administering reactionaire to participants at end of process___, using external evaluators___, gathering product measures___, monitoring processes systematically___, others (specify)_____.

4. How would you compare this P with others you have known with respect to his role in the planning and evaluating of events/projects/programs?

1	.	2	.	3	.	4	.	5
extremely ineffective								extremely effective

DATA SHEET: PROBLEM SOLVING

1. Name a problem that you think he handled well.

    How did it arise? (What events occurred?)

    What did he do?

    How was the problem resolved?

2. Name a problem that you think he did not handle well.

    How did it arise? (What events occurred?)

    What did he do?

    How was the problem resolved?

3. The P has probably had to deal with conflict between two or more
    adults. Recall a specific instance of this and describe what the
    P did.

4. How would you compare this P with others you have known, with
    respect to his ability as a solver of problems?

1	.	2	.	3	.	4	.	5
extremely								extremely
ineffective								effective

89

DATA SHEET: CHANGE

1. What major changes occurred in this high school during the past
    calendar year in which the P had a major role? curriculum___,
    management___, community relations___, staff relations___, student
    behavior___, student activities___, school climate___, others
    (specify) _____.

2. Where did the idea for (one of the above) originate? staff___,
    students___, patrons___, central administration___, advisory
    group___, principal___, others (specify) _____.

3. What is the P's typical role in the changes that occur in the high
    school here? initiator___, planner___, consultant___, facilitator___,
    evaluator___, others (specify) _____.

4. How would you compare this P with others you have known with
    respect to his role as a change agent?

    _____1_____.____2_____.____3_____.____4_____.____5_____
          extremely   extremely
          ineffective   effective

_____Number

DATA SHEET: PERSONAL/PROFESSIONAL

1. As far as you know, why was the P selected for the position in this
    high school?

2. What do you consider to be his major strengths/assets in handling the
    job?

3. What do you consider to be his limitations?

4. What types of things seem to "get to" the principal and cause him
    anxiety, stress, worry, etc.?

5. What do you see as the main institutional (school) and social
    (society) constraints which may handicap the principal in doing
    a good job?

6. How could the job of the principal be improved and made more effective?

7. What do you see as conditions, either within schools or in society,
    that are likely to have significant influence upon your school
    during the next three to five years? enrollment changes___,
    students' nonattendance___, alternative schools, programs___,
    demands for basics___, declining achievement___, compulsory educa-
    tion___, community-based learning___, national youth service___,
    desegregation___, finance & general economy___, drug use___,
    accountability___, new technology___, community participation___,
    staff competency___, competency testing___, graduation require-
    ments___, other (specify) _____.

90